The Dilemma of Northern Ireland

A HOUSE DIVIDED

The Dilemma of Northern Ireland

JAMES CALLAGHAN

Collins, St James's Place, London, 1973

William Collins Sons & Co Ltd
London · Glasgow · Sydney · Auckland
Toronto · Johannesburg

First published 1973
© James Callaghan, 1973

ISBN 0 00 211073 3

Set in Monotype Times
Made and printed in Great Britain by
William Collins Sons & Co Ltd Glasgow

To My Wife

And if a kingdom be divided against itself,
   that kingdom cannot stand.
And if a house be divided against itself,
   that house cannot stand.

Gospel According to St Mark,
Chapter 3, verses 24 and 25.

Foreword

I have to record my grateful thanks to many friends who have helped me with this book. To Maurice Edelman, MP, the first to persuade me that I could write it: to the officials who worked with me at the Home Office on Northern Ireland affairs and who have recently gone to immense trouble to meet my requests by disinterring the records of those fateful days and answering my questions. I thank especially Robin North and Neil Cairncross.

Among others I record my thanks to my daughter, Margaret Jay, who did some of the early research, and to John Clare for his numerous discussions with me and his patient work on the text.

I am particularly grateful to Merlyn Rees, MP, Labour Party spokesman on Northern Ireland affairs, and to Sir Philip Allen, former Permanent Under-Secretary at the Home Office, who read the manuscript and made many suggestions for improvement. He bears no responsibility for the text. Nor does William Whitelaw, the Secretary of State for Northern Ireland, whom I should also like to thank for agreeing to talk to me about the future.

Finally, my grateful thanks to Ruth Sharpe, who typed and corrected the manuscript with her accustomed skill and in complete disregard of normal working hours.

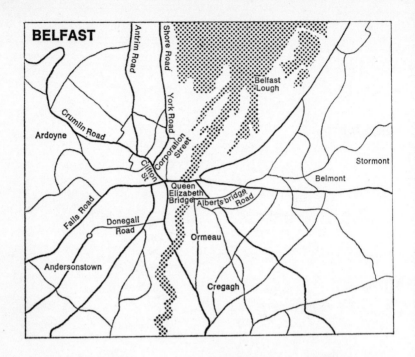

BELFAST

Antrim Road

Shore Road

York Road

Belfast Lough

Crumlin Road

Corporation Street

Ardoyne

Clifton St

Stormont

Queen Elizabeth Bridge

Belmont

Albertsbridge Road

Falls Road

Donegall Road

Ormeau

Andersonstown

Cregagh

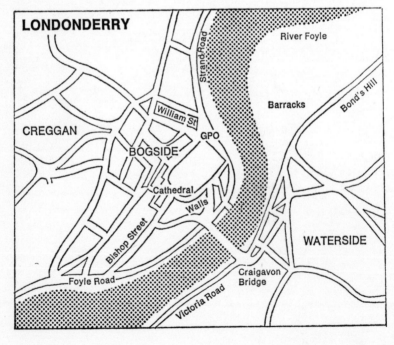

LONDONDERRY

Strand Road

River Foyle

William St

Barracks

Bond's Hill

CREGGAN

GPO

BOGSIDE

Cathedral

Walls

Bishop Street

WATERSIDE

Foyle Road

Craigavon Bridge

Victoria Road

1

It is almost impossible to open a newspaper, turn on the television or listen to the radio without hearing some account of disturbances, deaths, explosions, riots or political crises in Northern Ireland. It has become difficult, therefore, at this distance to recall just how little was the public attention paid to Northern Ireland at the time when I became Home Secretary in December 1967.

I can illustrate this by an anecdote concerning the first despatch box that was ever made up for me by my new Private Secretary on my first day in the office. I intended to be away from the Home Office for a few days so I asked for a series of documents on the problems that he thought would concern me most during my early weeks and months. When I opened the Box it contained books and papers about the future of the prison service, the fire service, problems on race relations, a number of questions about the police, children in care and their future, and the reform of the House of Lords—but not a word about Northern Ireland, although it was the concern of the Home Office. I was not surprised by this omission for the subject rarely, if ever, came before the Cabinet and its concerns had fallen into a settled routine at the Home Office itself.

A convention had grown up many years earlier that the government at Westminster did not interfere in Ulster's affairs. During the lifetime of the Attlee Government between 1945 and 1951, and again in the middle 1950s, small groups of Labour MPs used to raise questions about unemployment and civil rights in the Parliament at Westminster, but their attempts to do so were always jealously resented by the Ulster Unionist members who represented Northern Ireland and succeeding Speakers discouraged Questions to Ministers, and debates. After the 1964 Election, Paul Rose, the MP for Blackley, and Stanley Orme, MP for Salford West, led a new group of Labour MPs who persistently attempted to prise open Northern Ireland

1

problems, but they found great difficulty in doing so. Terence O'Neill, the Prime Minister of Northern Ireland from 1963-9, was very experienced and showed no particular enthusiasm for visits to the Province by Home Secretaries. In my early days I raised the question of a visit with O'Neill when he came to pay a courtesy call on me early in 1968, but he was plainly not very excited by the proposal and I let it drop.

Not surprisingly, the staff at the Home Office engaged on Northern Ireland affairs was extremely small. Indeed, Northern Ireland was crammed into what was called the General Department, which was responsible for anything which did not fit into any of the major departments of the Home Office. It covered such matters as ceremonial functions, British Summer Time, London taxicabs, liquor licensing, the administration of the state-owned pubs in Carlisle, and the protection of animals and birds. One Division also dealt with the Channel Islands, the Isle of Man, the Charity Commission and Northern Ireland, and this group of subjects was under the control of a staff of seven, of whom only one was a member of what was called the Administrative class. The day-to-day work and responsibility for Northern Ireland affairs was in the hands of my colleague and friend, Lord Stonham, who had been Parliamentary Under-Secretary and later became Minister of State at the Home Office. Northern Ireland was one of the main passions in his life and he coupled this with prison reform. He was on very good personal terms with Northern Ireland Ministers and Opposition MPs and the Northern Ireland civil service. There seemed to me at that time no reason to disturb the arrangement that I found on arrival. Besides, there were many other things to preoccupy me.

First there was the legislation on race relations to which my predecessor, Roy Jenkins, had rightly committed the Government. But none of the main principles or details had been decided by the Cabinet and one of my first tasks was to shape this legislation and take it through the various Committees. Another interest of mine was the care of children, which I had learned about from my wife's activities in this field. It seemed to me that reform was long overdue and should take place on the principle that the care of children and the control of children should go hand in hand instead of being divided between the courts and the local authorities. Another question which took up much time in the early months was the reform of the House of Lords. This was not a particularly palatable subject for me because George Brown and I had been the two members of the Cabinet most strongly opposed to the enterprise in the first place, but under the influence of Gerald Gardiner, the Lord Chancellor, and Dick Crossman, the Cabinet had agreed to set up a negotiating committee with the Conservative Party. I expected to find Dick Crossman's hammer and anvil approach to discussion unsuitable for negotiation and so I was surprised to find with what skill and sensitivity he handled Lord Carrington and Lord Jellicoe, as well as Iain Macleod and Reginald Maudling. However, despite Crossman's skill and enthusiasm, the odds were always strongly against the kind of reform that eventually emerged from the Committee. The Labour Party would not stand for it and there was no enthusiasm for it among the Conservative backbenchers. Moreover, Iain MacLeod himself had been very hostile to any reform prior to the next General Election, and I was not in the least surprised when the Bill had to be abandoned.

Another Bill that was in a very advanced state when I arrived at the Home Office was to control Betting and Gaming. This Bill has stood the test of time and enabled Sir Stanley Raymond and the Gaming Board to curb the activities of the Mafia and other near-criminal syndicates before they gained a serious foothold.

During the winter of 1967-8 I also had the problem of the Kenya Asians who had been emigrating to this country in large numbers for several months. I came under heavy criticism for introducing legislation to control the flow, but although heavy, the attack was not widespread and the legislation went through Parliament with very large majorities. This legislation took the heat out of immigration for some time.

Quite apart from these matters, there were the day-to-day problems which force themselves on the attention of the Home Secretary and which arise at great speed. They make the Home Office an extremely fascinating place in which to work. All questions concerned with the relationship between the law and the citizen, or problems of civil rights, arouse intense and very real concern among the public and in the Press, and the Home Secretary's own personal attention is frequently needed for an individual case. The question may concern a jail escape, or the problem of a child who has been treated badly at an Approved School, or it may be a matter of young people and drugs, or allegations of corruption against a policeman: these issues demand great care and often take up a lot of time. I found them absorbing and vital in my attempts to strike the right balance between the individual and the state.

So with all this I had no occasion to seek more work or to go out and look at the problems of Northern Ireland, unless they forced themselves upon me. I dare say that if the public had been asked their views on Northern Ireland at that time their answer would have been that it was known to be a development area with very heavy unemployment but whose politics were a hidden mystery.

The reality, of course, was very different. Captain O'Neill, the Prime Minister of Northern Ireland at the time, speaking after the troubles had broken out in 1968, said: 'The tinder for that fire in the form of grievances real or imaginary had been piling up for years.' What were these grievances? First, large numbers of Catholics had never reconciled themselves to the partition of the country that had been made at the time of the settlement of 1921 and looked more to Dublin than to Stormont as their capital. Next, the Ulster Unionist Government had been in power for more than fifty years, and was made up wholly of Protestants. There were no Catholic members of the Administration; there never had been; and there was hardly a Catholic member of the Unionist Party in the country. Because they were in a permanent minority the Catholic Opposition had no hope of ever forming a Government.

They excluded themselves from any share in government and, in addition, they were deliberately excluded by the Ulster Unionist majority. The Ulster Unionist Party was insensitive to the injustices that the minority suffered in such matters as electoral discrimination in voting and in fixing electoral boundaries, in housing allocations and in employment, especially by local authorities, although this was not so in central government.

Just as importantly, there was complete segregation of the communities in the spheres of education, social activities and religion. The communities mostly lived apart, each in its own housing area. Only in the trades unions and among the professional middle classes was there any real contact between Protestants and Catholics. The trades unions consistently endeavoured to operate on a non-sectarian basis and in 1966 drew up a memorandum asking that the law and the administration in Northern Ireland should be brought up to British standards, that there should be electoral reform to eliminate gerrymandering and to give every adult the vote, and that there should be measures to get rid of discrimination in employment, caused by politics or religion. A deputation was formed from the Irish Congress of Trade Unions, the Labour MPs in Stormont and the Northern Ireland Labour Party. Captain O'Neill, the Prime Minister, was ill and the deputation was received by Brian Faulkner, the Deputy Prime Minister, William Craig, who was the Minister for Home Affairs, and two other Ministers. The results of the interview were unsatisfactory but subsequently Captain O'Neill decided to abolish the business vote in local government elections and included it in his next programme. A little later a Civil Rights Association was formed – modest in numbers. Its founders' intention was that it should be non-sectarian; anyone was welcome if he or she accepted the basic principle of civil rights for all. It was basically a middle-class enterprise at the beginning of its history.

Tension had been caused by Captain O'Neill's belief that he could pull his own Party forward into the main stream of Conservative thinking in Britain and at the same time reconcile the Northern Catholics to the continued existence of the border by working more closely with the government of the Republic. To this end he exchanged visits with the Prime Minister of the Republic. This caused a reaction among many members of the Orange Order and advantage was taken of the trouble by the Rev. Ian Paisley, who affected to see that O'Neill was deserting the cause of Protestantism. The Rev. Paisley was also very much opposed to the attempt made by the Archbishop of Canterbury to achieve a better understanding with the Church of Rome. He thundered his denunciations with all the vigour and eloquence that he commands.

O'Neill would have made an excellent Prime Minister in the Conservative tradition in easier times. He had a genuine distaste for the narrow-minded sectarianism of Ulster politics and was the first Northern Ireland politician in the Ulster Unionist Party to recognize that the Province had to take into account the world that lay beyond its own borders. By making a point of visiting Roman

Catholic schools and institutions, he tried to behave like the Prime Minister of the whole of the province and not just the Prime Minister of the Protestants. He wanted to solve these problems himself and was deeply opposed to British interference in Northern Ireland affairs. He wrote that: 'The long history of Anglo-Irish relationships warns that sudden intervention by the United Kingdom may produce effects which no one can foresee.'

Nevertheless, Ministers at the Home Office, and Harold Wilson, grew more and more impatient as time went by, and the Unionist Government failed to put right civil grievances that would not have been tolerated in the rest of the United Kingdom, although they were hampered by the long-standing convention of non-interference in Northern Ireland affairs.

Even so, some kind of intervention by the government at Westminster became necessary after two civil rights demonstrations in the autumn of 1968. The first march at Dungannon was to protest against anti-Catholic discrimination in the allocation of houses. This passed off peacefully. The second demonstration at Londonderry was a catastrophe. When the Civil Rights Association proposed to march partly through a traditional Protestant area, the organizers of the Protestant Apprentice Boys then announced that they intended to hold a march following a similar route and ending at the same place. This clash gave Mr Craig the opportunity of prohibiting all processions in the Waterside Ward east of the River Foyle or within the city walls. In the end the Apprentice Boys' march did not take place, but it had been a useful ploy to obstruct the proposed route of the Civil Rights Association. The CRA said their purpose was to publicize demands for one man one vote, in local government elections, an end to discrimination in employment and housing, the repealing of the Special Powers Act and the disbanding of the B-Specials. The organizers, after much argument among themselves, decided to go ahead with the march despite the ban. The crowd marched right up to a police cordon drawn across the narrow street and as the head of the march reached the cordon the front line of police drew their batons, stepped forward a couple of paces, and attacked the leaders, including Gerry Fitt, the MP for Belfast. The crowd stood fast, and an impromptu meeting was held where they were, but confusion then broke out, and a series of attacks on the police and counter-attacks by them took place. The police were under orders to disperse the marchers and used their batons, so that the hemmed-in crowd were driven back down the hill against a lower cordon of police through which they all passed, running the gauntlet. There was an ugly scene in which bricks and stones were hurled at the police, despite the appeals of the leaders of the march for calm. The television cameras were present in force and pictures of the extraordinary scenes of violence and fighting were flashed around the world. Ulster had arrived in the headlines.

Why did the tinder which had lain around in a combustible state for so many years catch fire at this particular moment in 1968? The answer lies partly in the nature of the situation itself, but also partly in what was taking place in the rest of the world during that year. 1968 was the year of the students' revolt. At the Sorbonne and at Nanterre University in May 1968 the French students brought France to a momentary standstill. President Pompidou was moved to say: 'Everything must be rethought.' In China the Red Guards were staging their revolution. In Biafra, in Spain, in Jugoslavia and in Poland, there was revolt and violence. It was the year when Dubcek's human face was followed by the Russian invasion of Czechoslovakia. In Wales a tiny handful of extremists were using bombs and explosions to forward their aims.

Student unrest in the East coincided with student revolts in the West, but not for the same reasons. In the West the protests were against a consumer materialist society from which the students proclaimed they were alienated. In the East, the cry of the students was for the democratization of bureaucracy, and at times when Western and Eastern students met there was a clash of opinion between them. Danny Cohn Bendit proclaimed: 'We demand freedom of expression inside the faculty but we refuse it to pro-Americans.' This was unacceptable to leaders of students in Eastern Europe. In September 1968, J. Kavan, the leader of Prague students, commented: 'I have often been told by my friends in Western Europe that we are only fighting for bourgeois democratic freedoms. But somehow I cannot distinguish between capitalist freedoms and socialist freedoms. What I recognize are basic human freedoms.'

Western students coined a phrase 'institutional violence', by which they meant that they were justified in attacking any institutions in the West which in their view represented traditional authority and were therefore evil. London was not exempt from what was taking place in Chicago, Paris, Berlin, from Berkeley to Budapest. The slogan of the year was a loud chant of 'Ho, Ho, Ho Chi Minh' and it was echoed all the way from Tokyo to Grosvenor Square, while stars like Tariq Ali, Cohn Bendit and Rudi Dutschke, swept across the firmament only to disappear within a year or so. British universities did not escape. The happenings there led *The Times* to write pontifically at the end of the summer term of 1968 that there had been 'a collapse of order in English universities'. The Vice-Chancellors, unused to the rowdy scenes that were enacted on their campuses, sent an impressive deputation to see me, as Home Secretary, for advice on the best way to handle these matters. In March 1968 there were violent scenes in Grosvenor Square as a result of a 'demo' against the Vietnam war and a further gigantic march was planned for October 27th, 1968. This dreadful war not only divided American society but created great divisions in this country also. There was a crisis of conscience among many young people.

The great anti-Vietnam war march in London was due to take place only three weeks after the violent civil rights demonstration in Londonderry. I was put under great pressure in Parliament to ban it, and was solemnly warned by the Conservatives at Question Time that I would be held personally responsible for the serious disorder that might ensue if the march was not prohibited. Quintin Hogg came to see me at the Home Office and, his composure deserting him, proposed that I should confine the Guards to their London barracks so that they could be available to put down any revolt. He further suggested that I should close all the main line railway stations and have every car and coach coming into London searched. The Press and television helped to build up the expected horrors, and confirmed my opinion that however well intentioned they may be, the Press and television are not passive recorders of what they see. The normal is not news, only everything that is original, or strange, or extreme.

Under the pressure of publicity, apprehension built up and hotheads took advantage of the public fears to get even more publicity. Students occupied the London School of Economics, announcing that it would be used as a hospital for the wounded on the day of the demonstration. Parallels were drawn by the Press with the demonstrations in France the previous May in which the students had used fire bombs, and had attacked key buildings, and the French police had responded in their customary manner with prohibition, riot police and tear gas. We were solemnly told by foreign observers that the traditional methods used by the Metropolitan Police would not do on this occasion. I held a number of consultations with the Commissioner of Police for the Metropolis, Sir John Waldron, with Commander Lawlor, who was to be in operational control of the march, and other senior police officers and Home Office advisers. Both Sir John Waldron and I thought alike on this matter; we were both agreed that the march should go on and that the police should under-react and not over-react to events of the day. Our intention was that arrests should be minimized, because we knew that Tariq Ali and his associates were hoping that the police would maximize arrests and so help to create an atmosphere of martyrdom for the demonstrators.

The march on Sunday afternoon was very large. Thirty thousand people took part, according to the police estimate, and others put the figure very much higher. At a critical point in the afternoon some of the more violent marchers struck off and marched to Grosvenor Square, where they attempted to fight a pitched battle with the police. For some time it looked as though their tactics might pay off, but the police showed remarkable steadiness and under skilled leadership repulsed the violent attacks of the marchers. The day ended with the remnants of the marchers and the police singing 'Auld Lang Syne' as they broke off the engagement. The police emerged from the day with their reputation enhanced and rightly enjoyed very great public credit for the successful methods they had employed.

Elsewhere student unrest and demonstrations continued, for the most part from a genuine desire on the part of students to participate more in the decisions that affected their lives, but on the part of some of the extreme Left from a hankering after violence for its own sake.

It was against this world problem of violence and revolt that the October 5 march in Londonderry should be seen, and although there were deep-rooted and long-standing grievances also, I believe that what was happening elsewhere helped to set the Northern Ireland tinder aflame at that moment. Immediately after the riot, Harold Wilson sent an urgent invitation to Terence O'Neill to come to London to talk things over early in November. He did so bringing with him Brian Faulkner, the Deputy Prime Minister, William Craig, the Minister for Home Affairs, and Sir Harold Black, the Secretary to the Northern Ireland Cabinet. On our side were Wilson, Alice Bacon, then at the Ministry of Education, whom Wilson had brought in because she got on well with O'Neill, Sir Philip Allen, the Permanent Secretary at the Home Office, and myself.

The Prime Minister began by saying that there was deep concern in Britain about the disturbances in Londonderry and the underlying causes. We would prefer to reach agreement with the Northern Ireland Government but pressure was growing at Westminster. If the Ulster Cabinet could not introduce the necessary reforms, particularly in relation to the electoral laws and the Special Powers Act, we might have to apply sanctions such as reconsidering the financial arrangements between the two countries, or even changing their constitutional relationship. Wilson pointed out that whereas the twelve Ulster MPs at Westminster could vote against the Government and even defeat it, we could not even debate Northern Ireland at Westminster. He did not spell it out at the time but what he had in mind was cutting off Northern Ireland's representation at Westminster.

I pointed out that the violence would inevitably grow if the Northern Ireland Government refused to meet legitimate political demands. I felt the greatest need for improvement was probably in the provision of more jobs, but we felt very strongly that there was a need, too, for a fair housing system and in particular a code of conduct in the allocation of housing that all local authorities should be required to adhere to. Plural company voting and the property qualification provisions in the local government franchise were also emotive issues and ought to be changed quickly. Finally, I said that where there was only the possibility of one-party government the need for an Ombudsman was all the greater. O'Neill then invited Craig to tell us what he thought.

Craig said that 74 local authorities for a population of 1,500,000 were far too many and the Government was therefore proposing a radical reduction in their numbers and functions. He said reform in the electoral laws would have to wait on this new local government structure which might take two or three years, and anyway reform might not be necessary if the new authorities' responsibilities were to be reduced. Also, he added, new houses were being built all the time, which meant that more and more people would meet the property qualification. Wilson and I both said we were disappointed by this approach: why should we wait?

Craig said the housing allocation system worked smoothly. There were no more than a dozen complaints a year. Also, in his view, there was no need for an Ombudsman because conditions in Northern Ireland were very different from those in Britain, a view with which we both agreed! Craig thought that a grave situation was building up because of a recrudescence of IRA activity. The IRA, he said, played a big part in the civil rights movement and so repeal of the Special Powers Act was out of the question. Finally, he could not possibly agree to an inquiry into what had happened in Londonderry in October: he had gone into the matter and had complete confidence in the measures taken by the police.

About two weeks after he had returned home O'Neill announced his conclusions. There were to be widespread changes. Council houses would be allotted on a basis of need and in accordance with a clear points system; a Bill would be brought in to appoint an Ombudsman, and machinery for investigating complaints against local authorities and other public bodies would be considered; local government would be reformed by the end of 1971, and with it the franchise; controversial sections of the Special Powers Act would be withdrawn as soon as it was possible to do so; and the Londonderry Borough Council, which was widely regarded as corrupt, would be replaced by a development commission.

Early in December he made a powerful appeal on television to the people of Ulster to support these policies. The response was overwhelming. Nearly 150,000 people signed messages and declarations of support. He also received a huge vote of confidence from his Party and I think overestimated his strength as a result. He said in his broadcast that he was aware that some foolish people had been asking why they should bow the knee to a Labour Prime Minister and why not hold out until a Conservative Government returned to power. 'My friends,' he said, 'that is a delusion.' Then, waving a letter, he went on: 'This letter is from Mr Edward Heath and tells me with the full authority of the Shadow Cabinet and the express support of my old friend Sir Alec Douglas-Home that the reversal of the policies which I have tried to pursue would be every bit as unacceptable to the Conservative Party. If we adopt an attitude of stubborn defiance we will not have a friend left at Westminster . . . Mr Wilson made it absolutely clear to us that if we did not face up to our problems the Westminster Parliament might well decide to act over our heads. Where would our constitution be then? What shred of self-respect would be left to us if we allowed others to solve our problems because we have not the guts – let me use a plain word – the guts to face up to them? We would be utterly shamed.' Craig made a series of speeches in Northern Ireland at this period which seemed to criticize O'Neill's policies, and accordingly O'Neill sacked him shortly after his broadcast.

There then followed the civil rights march over the New Year from Belfast to Londonderry. The march itself was ill-advised, but that was no excuse for the ambush of about 500 marchers at Burntollet Bridge by 200 Protestant extremists who most ferociously attacked them. That night groups of policemen, a few of whom had had too much to drink, charged into the Bogside, the Catholic area of Derry. The verdict on their behaviour was given later in the year by a Commission of Enquiry headed by Lord Cameron, who was appointed by O'Neill to examine the causes and nature of the violence and disturbances, and who found that 'a number of policemen were guilty of misconduct which involved assault and battery, and malicious damage to property.'

I thought that a pretty cool account of what appeared to have been a major breakdown in discipline, of a kind which would not have been tolerated in a British police force. Altogether 163 people were treated in hospital after that weekend.

Following the dismissal of Craig, the next event to shake the O'Neill Government was the resignation of Faulkner, the Deputy Prime Minister, on 23 Jan. 1969. The reason he gave was the appointment of the Cameron Commission to investigate the causes of the riots. He said that the Government itself should have decided what ought to be done and the Administration was falling down on its policy. No doubt Faulkner felt this, but there is equally no doubt that during much of O'Neill's Government he had been seeking an opportunity to replace him as Prime Minister. Indeed in his letter of reply, O'Neill referred to the numerous occasions on which he should have had loyalty and support from Faulkner, but such loyalty and support had been absent and he had not been in the forefront in defending the Administration. In my view O'Neill was convinced of the need for change and reform but was very dubious of his capacity to carry his parliamentary party with him. He therefore hoped that the Cameron Report, when it was published, would be a means to persuade those of his Party who would not otherwise agree.

However, he was not to remain Prime Minister for long enough to see this happen. Faulkner's resignation revealed the divisions within the Unionist Party and a few days later, 12 of the dissident Unionist MPs met in Portadown and demanded the removal of O'Neill from the leadership. O'Neill responded by calling a General Election, hoping that by an appeal to the electorate for middle ground support he would be able to carry his programme through. But the results of that election, held on February 24, were only marginally less confusing than the election itself. Many Unionist constituency parties split into pro- and anti-O'Neill factions. O'Neill won, but it was a long way short of the decisive victory he needed. Added to which, he came uncomfortably close to being defeated in his own Bannside constituency by the Rev. Ian Paisley.

What finally sealed O'Neill's fate was a remarkable series of five explosions at electricity and water installations during March and April 1969. At the time they were unhesitatingly, inevitably and inaccurately described by the Royal Ulster Constabulary as the work of the IRA. Later it transpired that they were perpetrated by members of the Ulster Volunteer Force, an extreme Protestant body outlawed by O'Neill three years earlier. They were remarkable because their purpose was to topple O'Neill from power by creating the false impression that the IRA had a stranglehold on the country's essential services and that O'Neill could not control them, and to secure the release from prison of Paisley and Paisley's right-hand man, Major Ronald Bunting, both serving six-month sentences for taking part in an unlawful assembly. Both aims were to be triumphantly realized. O'Neill resigned on April 28, three days after the last explosion – at the Silent Valley reservoir, which cut off two-thirds of Belfast's water supply for 10 days – and Paisley and Bunting were released under a general amnesty announced on May 6. The explosions also led to British troops being called out to guard key installations.

Later a former B-Special, Samuel Stevenson, who admitted being involved in three of the raids, was jailed for twelve years. Five other men, against whom he gave evidence, were all acquitted by Belfast juries.

A few days before O'Neill resigned there had been a curious development: he won a vote of confidence from his parliamentary party for his proposed electoral reform, but Major James Chichester-Clark, who had been Minister of Agriculture, resigned from the Government – ostensibly on the ground that the timing of this decision was wrong. There was speculation that the move, whether intended or not, was in reality a ploy to ensure that the succession did not go to Faulkner whose opponent was none other than Chichester-Clark. Chichester-Clark won by one vote, and later O'Neill made no secret of the fact that he considered that one vote to be his own.

Chichester-Clark, who is a distant cousin of O'Neill's and shares his background of Eton and the Irish Guards, immediately made clear that he intended to implement all the reforms promised by O'Neill, including the one which had apparently caused him to resign. Such is the way of Irish politics.

Meanwhile, Bernadette Devlin had been elected to Westminster at a by-election in Mid-Ulster and, in the wake of renewed rioting in Londonderry, made a dramatic and eloquent maiden speech. It was certainly the most eloquent maiden speech I had ever heard, and in replying to the debate I congratulated her on it but added that it was wholly unconstructive and negative. Almost everyone else, however, including all the British Press, was busy worshipping at the altar. In later debates most of the House turned against her, but she showed great determination in outfacing their serried ranks and I know few more unnerving experiences than facing a united and hostile House of Commons; nevertheless, she pressed on.

The first test for Chichester-Clark came with the Orange marches on July 12, 1969, the day when upwards of 100,000 Protestants commonly take to the streets all over Northern Ireland to celebrate the victory of William of Orange over the Catholic King James II at the Battle of the Boyne in 1690. Rioting between Catholics and Protestants broke out in Belfast and Londonderry, where it lasted for two nights, and in the predominantly Catholic town of Dungiven, where a mob set fire to the local Orange hall. One hundred and fifty troops were moved to Londonderry and put on stand-by duty, but the police managed to retain control and an uneasy peace ensued. In London we were debating whether we should intervene, but hoping and praying that we would not have to. The advice that came to me from all sides was on no account to get sucked into the Irish bog. For the time being we decided we would wait.

2

The next outbreak of violence was not long in coming. It happened as so often before at a weekend, on August 2. But on this occasion there were some new and unwelcome features. The usual pattern was for the riots to start on Saturday night, intensify when the pubs closed, fade away on Sunday morning, flare up again on Sunday evening, and subside in the early hours of Monday. Throughout all these troubles, it was remarkable how little working time was lost.

Ominously, on this first weekend of August, the riots which started on Saturday and continued on Sunday spilled over into Monday night and Tuesday. Equally ominous was the fact that Belfast was the scene of the trouble, and those with long memories – and who in Ireland has not? – knew only too well that when a Belfast mob gets out of hand, it is more fanatical and destructive than any in outlying areas. It was over thirty years since there had been other than relatively minor and isolated rioting in the city. Now it had arrived on a grand scale.

I heard the news with some gloom and, as the details accumulated, it became clear that there was yet another new factor. This rioting had little to do with the marches and demonstrations for civil rights; it seemed to have more of the flavour of the old-fashioned 'Prod versus Mick' punch-up. According to the reports that came to me the rioting started when a group of junior Orangemen due to rally in other parts assembled complete with bands and drums at the bottom of the Shankill Road, close to a block of flats misnamed Unity Walk and mainly occupied by Roman Catholics. The two groups were within throwing distance of each other and the almost inevitable happened. At the time nobody could tell me who threw the first stones. Although the Scarman Commission of Enquiry into these events later found that the Protestants were the aggressors, such information was far less important that weekend than the fact

16

that there were hundreds of people ready to carry on and intensify the battle once the engagement had started.

By evening, when the bands had come marching home, every window in the front of Unity Walk was broken and the residents had retreated from the front of the block. Some extremist youths, who called themselves Protestants, looked as though they might try to break into the flats and at this stage the police, wearing their riot kit of crash helmets, visors and shields, very properly tried to disperse them. They baton-charged and there was a running fight. The Protestants were obviously taken aback by this, and later the Protestant Shankill Defence Association declared that the police were 'no longer the friends of Ulster Loyalists and can never expect our help again'. By midnight nearly 100 people had been injured. On Sunday Paisley came to the scene and was obviously dismayed by what was taking place. He urged the crowd to go to church or go home, but his appeal was unsuccessful. His colleague, Major Bunting, was booed and had stones thrown at him when he tried to persuade the crowd to disperse.

I took the view that there were a lot of drunken hooligans on the streets on both nights, who were egged on by a small group of ultra Protestants, anxious that there should be trouble. The police, a number of whom were injured, made nearly 50 arrests.

Again, when the violence started on Monday night it was difficult to know who struck the first blow, but as rival mobs of Protestants and Roman Catholics fought with petrol bombs and bottles, there was little doubt that it was the Catholic areas which suffered most. Indeed, while the police struggled to keep the groups apart, it seemed as though a number of Protestant youths were acting as a kind of commando force.

The events of the night highlighted one of the basic weaknesses of the police: there were simply not enough of them to handle hooliganism and disorder on such a scale. Their total strength throughout Ulster and Belfast was no more than 3000 to control a province of over 5000 square miles and to protect a million and a half people. Making allowances for the fact that they needed rest periods and were working in three shifts round the clock, there were usually less than 1000 police available for duty during any normal shift, and unlike the English police they could not be reinforced by neighbouring Forces. On the Sunday and Monday evenings in Belfast, only a few hundred policemen were on duty. By contrast, a large demonstration on a Sunday afternoon in London may be covered by 3000 to 4000 policemen, and at the Vietnam demonstration in Grosvenor Square in October 1968, there were over 9000 policemen on duty along the route. There was a pathetic inadequacy about the number of RUC men available.

A maximum strength of 3000 had been fixed in the original Northern Ireland Act as long ago as 1922, and although any limit on the maximum was removed in 1963, the Northern Ireland Government made no attempt to increase the total. In conversations with the Ministers in the Northern Ireland Government during the winter of 1968 and the spring of 1969, I had pressed that recruitment should be increased and that an effort should be made to get more Catholics into the force. I was told then that the Northern Ireland Government hoped to reach an expanded total of 3200 by 1975 – an addition of only 40 per year. I regarded this target as totally inadequate, and the Minister of Home Affairs knew my view. But the target was adhered to and no attempt was made to increase the rate of recruitment, apparently because the Northern Ireland Government did not want to spend the extra money. So the rioting spread, and the strain on the force, which was overstretched to start with, grew without respite. It was simply too small to cope.

The situation was, of course, further complicated by the lack of trust that the Catholic section of the population felt in the RUC, whom they regarded as being basically orientated towards the Protestant section of the community and the Ulster Unionist Government. The truth is somewhat mixed. There were, undoubtedly, a number of policemen, some in key positions, who strongly sympathized with the Protestants, but most of the force wanted to do an impartial job and looked with envy at the purely civil role of British police forces. Unfortunately, the leadership never gave them a real opportunity to pursue that role.

There were also insuperable difficulties about using the Ulster Special Constabulary – the B-Specials – which was about 8000 strong. In private life, its members were farmers and shopkeepers who had volunteered for special constabulary duties, but they were completely untrained in crowd control and were a wholly Protestant force. They had originally been established in 1920 to defend the border with the South and not to carry out police duties, and their training was primarily of a military nature. Seen by the Protestants as their shield against the IRA, they were not Special Constables in the sense in which the term is used in the rest of the United Kingdom. Although they were acceptable in the Protestant areas for patrol purposes, in the atmosphere of Northern Ireland at the time they were quite unacceptable for the purpose of keeping Catholics and Protestants apart in the factional riots that broke out.

The events of that weekend caused Paul Rose, the MP for Manchester, Blackley, who was chairman of the Campaign for Democracy in Ulster, to urge me publicly to relieve the Northern Ireland Government of the control of the RUC and to take it over personally. Naturally, his proposal was immediately repudiated by Robert Porter, who had taken over as Minister of Home Affairs. Bernadette Devlin also asked me to put the RUC in the hands of senior British police officers. But to take control of the RUC at that time, without any preparation and without any idea of how the force itself would react to such a proposition, against the will of the Ulster Unionist Government and without sufficient policemen to do what was necessary, would have made the situation worse rather than better. There was also a suggestion that British police should be called upon to reinforce the RUC, but until the Police Act 1970 there was no legal provision by which this could be done, and the British police objected in principle to serving when the Special Powers Act was in force. There would have been a lot of opposition from the Police Federation to their members being placed under the direct control of the Northern Ireland Minister of Home Affairs, and therefore outside the overall responsibility of the Home Secretary. In many ways I was sorry about this because some of the larger British police forces, especially the Metropolitan, have built up considerable experience in methods of handling demonstrations and crowds and, despite the great differences between Britain and Northern Ireland, I felt they could have been of value.

As all this was ruled out, the only remaining force, in the event of the RUC being overrun, was the British Army. There were substantial disadvantages in calling them in. Quite apart from the sensitivity that would be aroused south of the border, and to some extent in the North itself, Army units were not specifically trained for crowd control, even though some of their commanders had had experience in Cyprus. The men themselves were much younger than the average policeman, with less experience of civilian life, and they had no experience of Irish history or passions. We knew it would be a thankless task for them, and Denis Healey, who was Secretary of State for Defence, was naturally reluctant to commit forces in this way unless it was shown that there was no alternative. I agreed with him and in the discussions before the event there was no disposition on my part to push him to do so. But by August 2, the nature and extent of the rioting, including the fact that it was spreading from Londonderry to Belfast and involving Protestant rioters, made the Home Office feel that the time was very close when we would have to face this issue.

Accordingly my officials at the Home Office were not surprised when they received an emergency call from the Northern Ireland Government on Sunday evening, August 3, asking what the response would be if they needed troops. I was immediately telephoned in the country and, following conversations between the Prime Minister in the Scilly Isles and myself, the Home Office officials told the Secretary to the Northern Ireland Cabinet the same evening that we gave agreement in principle to the use of troops. So simply was a momentous decision taken. They were also told that Denis Healey had called for on-the-spot reports and if, as a result of these, we reached the conclusion that the police could no longer hold the situation, then troops would be sent in.

The Northern Ireland Cabinet, who met each day during the weekend, were informed of this but I do not think they realized for some time what a far-reaching step they were proposing. Moreover, the Prime Minister, Chichester-Clark, remained on holiday in Switzerland and was not due back for another two or three days. The Northern Ireland Cabinet seemed to be under the impression that troops could be called in to take any necessary action, including shooting at crowds if need be, and when they had restored a sullen peace could be withdrawn to barracks, only to come back again if required to deal with further rioting.

I did not see it in this way. Once British troops had been committed, the Secretary of State for Defence would become responsible at Westminster for their conduct, their tactics and their policy. We would be put in the position of underwriters to a Government which up to that moment had shown little appreciation of the extent to which Britain and other parts of the world had been stirred by the television films and press photographs of what was going on. Moreover, I was certain that politically it would be a grave mistake to put British troops under the authority of the Ulster Unionist Government. Practically the whole of the Catholic population was by now thoroughly roused, and if the British Army were to appear to be an arm of the Ulster Unionist Government, the Catholics in their turn were likely to regard the troops with the same distaste as they regarded their Government. I had no intention of putting British troops in this position and that could be avoided only if it were known and acknowledged that they remained under the control of the British Government. There was a further factor: it is easy enough to start something but much more difficult to call it off. I had seen this at first hand when the Conservative Government transported Archbishop Makarios from Cyprus to the Seychelles and we watched them wriggle for months to find a suitable reason for releasing him.

C'est le premier pas qui coûte. Denis Healey expressed this view very strongly, and we were both at odds with the Northern Ireland Government who thought that the troops could go in, undertake a short, sharp action, and then withdraw. I recall that in the course of our discussions, Healey forecast that it would be at least two years before the troops could be withdrawn – and events were to prove that even that was optimistic.

It was true that British troops had been used in Ulster to quell riots on previous occasions, for example in 1935. The intervention then had been short-lived, but the circumstances now were entirely different. For one thing, the Ulster Unionist Government was weaker in personnel and in public standing than it had been thirty years earlier. It had been severely shaken by internal convulsions, including the recent replacement of the Prime Minister. The Catholic minority were more enraged than they had ever been before, and Britain and the world knew more of what was going on and regarded it with a certain sense of horror. Indeed, I was told that the Conservative Central Office received a larger post bag at that time than on any other issue, particularly asking why the Conservative Party was linked with the Ulster Unionist Party.

A further factor was that Lord Cameron and his colleagues were on the point of concluding their investigations into the disturbances of the previous winter, and when the report was published it seemed likely to be very critical of the Northern Ireland Government. We would have been placed in an impossible position if British troops were committed to Northern Ireland for a substantial period while the Ulster Unionist Government sat behind British bayonets and failed to make the necessary changes. Such a position could never endure and I do not believe that any of the parties in the British Parliament would have supported it. The only major dissent came from the *Daily Telegraph*, whose editorials were highly idiosyncratic throughout the troubles and seemed basically concerned to voice the views of the Ulster Unionists and no one else.

None of us could foresee what consequences might flow from the introduction of British troops into Ulster to keep order. The more the Northern Ireland authorities insisted that trouble in Belfast and other towns ought to be treated in exactly the same way as if it were an outbreak of violence in Newcastle, Birmingham or Liverpool, the more clear it was to me that in such unlikely circumstances, the British Government and Parliament would not leave it to the local aldermen and councillors but would insist on taking control. So while the Army commanders were alerted about the possibility of their involvement and plainclothes soldiers appeared quietly on the streets in trouble spots to size up the situation, I asked the Home Office officials to convey to their opposite numbers in the Northern Ireland Government the possible consequences that could result from such a dramatic move. I warned them that in extreme circumstances it could lead to a suspension of the Government at Stormont – and this eventually took place in March 1972. I wished them to be under no illusions about this, but equally the officials made clear that the last thing I would want would be to take over the Government of Northern Ireland. At that stage we knew little enough at first hand about what was going on, and had few reliable means of finding out. We had no idea what the attitude of the RUC would be if such a drastic step became necessary, nor did we know with certainty whether we could expect the loyal services of the Northern Ireland civil servants, though before long both uncertainties were happily removed. Then again, might both majority and minority communities turn on the British Army?

On my initiative, contingency plans had been drawn up in the winter of 1968 making provision for the government of Northern Ireland in the event of the dismissal of the Northern Ireland Government. A Bill was drafted giving legal sanction to the actions we would have to take, and a number of alternative plans were considered. We carefully scrutinized the Government of Ireland Act 1920 and particularly Section 75. This said: 'Notwithstanding the establishment of the Parliaments of Southern and Northern Ireland ... or anything contained in this Act, the supreme authority of the Parliament of the United Kingdom shall remain unaffected and undiminished over all persons, matters and things in Ireland and every part thereof.' Our view was that in the last resort this section gave the Parliament at Westminster supreme authority to withdraw such powers as it had delegated.

The Northern Ireland Government were not privy to the details of our contingency plans because we wanted to avoid inducing excessive gloom in O'Neill when he was fighting for his political life. But the fact that I considered a suspension of Stormont might become necessary if they were unable to govern was conveyed to them, and I was not surprised when they reacted strongly. After all, for nearly fifty years they had been able to go their own way with virtually no interference from the United Kingdom Government. As the years had gone by, the convention had become cast iron that Westminster did not normally discuss affairs that were within the province of the Northern Ireland Government. So they had felt themselves free to act, or fail to act, in any way that suited their majority without regard to opinion in this country or the authority of the British Government. In fact, while proclaiming their strict loyalty to the United Kingdom, they had won more and more independence and were getting the best of both worlds.

Their position had also been strengthened by the Labour Government's declaration in 1949 that their constitutional relationship with the South could not be changed except with the consent of the Northern Ireland Parliament. This had, in fact, been embodied in the statute recognizing the full independence of the Republic of Ireland.

Now the Northern Ireland Cabinet were told for the first time since 1922 that they were not masters in their own house, as they had supposed, and the Secretary to the Cabinet, Sir Harold Black, flew from Belfast urgently on Tuesday, August 5 to have talks with Home Office officials. So far as I could ascertain, the attitude of the Northern Ireland Government was that the responsibilities of the British Government were limited to armed intervention for the purpose of preserving law and order, whereas what domestic policies they followed were their own affair. I could not accept this line of argument. Law and order, as it is called, spring out of the policies followed by a government and if it is to be acceptable to, and obeyed by, the great majority of citizens, they must acquiesce in the policies on which the Government rests. Our statute book is littered with laws that have failed because considerable sections of the population either ignored or disowned them. Discretion is then the better part of valour because attempts to enforce them lead either to disaster or to ridicule.

During the previous twelve months, the civil rights movement had skilfully concentrated on grievances that were real and very emotive, with the consequence that the authority of the Unionist Government was being steadily eroded among a substantial section of the population. It was unthinkable in these circumstances that either the British Government or Parliament would have supported a proposal to hand over British troops to prop up a régime which had lost so much authority, unless reforms were made.

Harold Black's instructions were to try to limit the degree of Westminster intervention, and he took the familiar line that once troops were committed, the limit of HMG's responsibility was the preservation of law and order. He pressed this hard at the Home Office; both Philip Allen, the Permanent Secretary, and Robin North, the Assistant Secretary, who had great experience and knowledge of Northern Ireland affairs, were fully aware of my views.

As no reliable alternative instrument of government existed, it seemed to me to be better to win the agreement of the Ulster Unionists to what was necessary than to use the power of Parliament to dismiss them. I had no confidence that if the Ulster Unionist Government were replaced British intervention in Irish affairs would make the situation better in the long run. These are quicksands for the British and I had adhered steadfastly to my view that the people living in Ireland had to come to terms with each other about the basis on which they were going to live together. But although I had no enthusiasm to be drawn in, nevertheless, if necessary, we should have to be.

All this was patiently explained to Harold Black, and having seen Home Office officials in action, I had no doubt that they did it with the maximum of diplomacy and tact in order to avoid unnecessarily wounding the feelings of the Northern Ireland Government. Nevertheless, Black had to return to Northern Ireland without having got the satisfaction his Cabinet were seeking.

Perhaps one point that we did not labour enough with Black was that there was nothing novel in the Government's attitude. In the last crisis-ridden days when O'Neill was Prime Minister, he and I had gone over this same ground, and there was a clear assumption on his part, without any prompting from me, that the use of British troops on an extended scale would lead almost inevitably to a *de facto* takeover. Perhaps he did not say so to his Cabinet. However, the Northern Ireland Government was obviously taken aback by the firmness of our position and the possible unpleasant consequences for themselves. It seemed to me that they ignored the reality that any day they might find themselves in a situation over which they had altogether lost control.

By this time Chichester-Clark had returned from his holiday. He telephoned me in Sussex and we had to speak on an open Post Office line. Our conversation was consequently somewhat guarded and not very fruitful, particularly since I had not then read some of the newspaper speculation about the constitutional position. Apparently a report in the *Financial Times* had powerfully influenced Chichester-Clark. This said British troops would be used to restore law and order only if the Northern Ireland Government first agreed to surrender its political authority to Westminster. Chichester-Clark obviously thought that this was an inspired leak. If it was, it had not come from me. In the course of the conversation I referred back in guarded terms to my earlier talks with O'Neill. What had passed between us then seemed to come as a surprise to Chichester-

Clark. I also indicated in general terms what I thought to be the effect of Section 75 on the constitutional relationship between the two Parliaments.

James Chichester-Clark is a very even-tempered man and rarely lets his emotions show. I always found him good to deal with because he was absolutely straight and usually came to the point without much embroidery. Whatever differences we had about powers or policies were never personalized because I respected and liked him. However, on this occasion, it was clear to me that he was very concerned at the prospect of any change in the relationship between the two Governments, as indeed I was myself. Later I had consultations with Philip Allen and other Home Office officials, who had travelled down to my home in Sussex from London. It was agreed that I should try to get Chichester-Clark away from a discussion of the legal and constitutional position and on to the more practical issues that would arise once troops were committed. As I said to him, we were getting closer to a situation in which the Northern Ireland Government might find itself unable to govern if rioting by both communities resulted in a breakdown of the administrative machine. The only body strong enough to restore peace in such a situation would be the British Army.

In the veiled discussion that went on in the British Press about this matter, the only significant voice raised to dispute the claim that British troops must be responsible to the British Cabinet and to no one else was, once again, the *Daily Telegraph*, which, in an editorial, expressed its view that the direction of British troops, subject to a UK veto, should be controlled by the Northern Ireland Government, and that they must be used simply and solely for the purpose of restoring peace.

In the course of a second telephone conversation with Chichester-Clark on the evening of August 6, I spelled out the impossibility of the *Daily Telegraph* line. I was quite determined not to accept it, although ready to go a long way in order not to appear publicly to be undermining the Northern Ireland Government. On the other hand, I was convinced that policy changes had to be made and that the Ulster Unionist majority, which had ruled unchallenged for so long in Stormont, must be brought to see this. Indeed, the fact that they might have to rely on British troops to maintain their government meant that they had no alternative but to jettison some of their independence.

I told Chichester-Clark that the current situation did not encourage me to think that if troops were called in it would be a short, sharp operation, perhaps dealing with some hooliganism, followed by their withdrawal and return to barracks. Once they were used, the operation was almost certain to be prolonged.

Chichester-Clark pressed once more for acceptance of the view that the British Government should remain responsible for law and order and leave the rest to Stormont, and so the conversation ended with disagreement between us. He never did make plain what he meant by 'law and order'.

The Northern Ireland Prime Minister did not leave the matter there. That same evening, he wrote me a long letter on the subject, and followed it up with a visit by himself and Robert Porter, the Minister of Home Affairs, to the Home Office on August 8. He played what he knew was his strongest card by emphasizing that if the British Government did step in, we would be taking on an open-ended commitment. He knew our reluctance to assume that. He stressed that the people of Northern Ireland were determined to have their own government at Stormont and that in this they were as serious as the South had been in 1919. I ought to consider, he said, how the British Government had failed to cope with Sinn Fein then. I assumed the implication of this was that the suspension of Stormont might lead to the sort of rebellion that the British Government had had to deal with from 1919 to 1921, only this time it would be the Ulster Volunteer Force who would be doing the shooting rather than the IRA.

We did not break much new ground on the constitutional position. I stuck to my view that the continuing use of British troops would make political intervention inevitable. For that reason, among others, I was as anxious as ever to avoid the direct involvement of British troops. Nevertheless, I said that a government which could not control the streets or the population was not a government in our understanding of the word. The Northern Ireland Government argued that, in common law, civilian authorities – for example, magistrates in Britain – could call upon the Army for assistance in preserving the peace. Was not the same thing true in

Northern Ireland? I did not regard this common law obligation as helping us in the political situation in which we found ourselves. If British troops had to be called in to keep the peace in an English city, it was highly unlikely that the ensuing situation would be left to the local magistrates to deal with. The central government at Westminster would come into play immediately. Ministers would intervene, the causes of the riots would be investigated and scrutinized, and Parliament would insist on the central government taking charge of a situation in which British troops might have been forced to fire on British civilians in a British city. It was impossible to imagine such a situation in Northern Ireland without the powers of the Northern Ireland Government being called into question. Moreover, there was the position of the Republic of Ireland to be considered. It could be anticipated that if British troops were used, the Government of the Republic of Ireland would probably raise the issue at the United Nations, where there is always a latent sympathy among some nations for anyone with a grievance against the United Kingdom. We had no doubt that we would be able to argue successfully that this was a domestic matter. But that argument in itself, especially with the eyes of the world upon us, meant that we would have to show that the Government at Westminster was effectively able to intervene, control the situation and introduce policies that would remove the causes of the revolt.

The Northern Ireland Prime Minister said he was in a difficult position: if they had to consider the political consequences of the use of troops, it might lead to delay in calling them in when they were needed. I said I was quite sure he would not delay in taking such a step if it would save lives, no matter what political situation might develop from it. It seemed that one argument that weighed heavily on him was his apprehension that the suspension of the Northern Ireland Parliament would remove the safeguard against a forcible union with the Republic. I then tried to get him on to matters of more immediate concern.

We discussed a number of questions concerning the police. At earlier encounters in May both with him and the Minister of Home Affairs I had several times urged that the RUC were substantially under strength, either by comparison with forces in Britain or with the needs of Northern Ireland, and I now returned to this subject. Porter said that the Northern Ireland Government were now budgeting for an increase of 100 men a year from 1970-5, which would bring the total strength up to 3500 in five years' time. I said somewhat brusquely that this was far too slow and that the Government ought to be aiming at a total of 3500 within a twelvemonth. I offered some senior officers from Great Britain to assist with training and organization. The offer was not taken up, but neither was it rejected; both Ministers were clearly concerned with the impact of such arrivals on the morale of the RUC. I appreciated their anxiety but it seemed to me that the situation was far too serious to allow that to be the prime consideration.

A further question inevitably followed. Because of the weakness of the RUC and their inability to cope with a number of riots breaking out at the same time in different areas, the Prime Minister and the Minister of Home Affairs asked us to agree to the use of other riot control methods, namely CS gas. They had been supplied with the old and dangerous CM gas some years earlier, but it had not been used. We were very troubled because at that moment persuasive attempts were being made on the international scene to outlaw the use of gas and I certainly had no desire to weaken these attempts. But in the absence of more policemen we were faced with a choice of evils. The use of CS gas might enable the RUC to control riots and so obviate the need to call in troops. That would have been an advantage in itself. We therefore laid down stringent conditions for the use of the gas. They were as follows: it could be used only if the rioting was substantial and was causing injury to persons and extensive damage to property; there must be a likelihood that the rioting would be prolonged; the gas itself must be used on a minimum scale; and the Inspector-General of the RUC and his advisers must be clear that it was the most humane way of bringing the situation under control.

In the event, the condition that the gas should be used on a minimum scale was not, in my view, strictly observed, although it is only fair to add that this happened at a time when the police were tired out and the command was not as strict as it should have been. Later I discovered that the scientists did not know as much about the effects of the gas as I had thought and in the light of information that was sent to me and which appeared in the news-papers, I set up an expert committee under the chairmanship of Sir Harold Himsworth. He prepared two reports, the first of which came quickly and said that there was no evidence to show that any healthy person was made ill or any sick person made permanently worse by exposure to the gas. However, the team recommended a wider investigation into the possible effects of CS gas on children, old people and the sick. They reported a year later that only in quite exceptional circumstances would people receive large enough doses of the gas to cause serious injury or death and that it was highly improbable that such conditions could arise in civil opera-tions with disciplined troops or policemen. They recommended that where CS gas was used in built-up areas care should be taken to ensure that missiles did not inadvertently enter rooms. The first report was alarming enough and immediately it had been studied I approved amendments to the code to control the use of the gas even more stringently. Nevertheless, despite its potential ill effects, it was obviously preferable to shooting.

3

While these important exchanges were taking place between the Northern Ireland Cabinet and ourselves, there was a lull in the Belfast streets. Most of the city went about its business normally, and the casual observer would have found it almost impossible to sense the tension that lay just beneath the surface: but it was there, despite the sincere and well meant attempts to keep the temperature down. Groups of Roman Catholics and Protestants joined together and, wearing arm bands for identification, toured the streets holding a series of meetings in the riot areas wherever they were able to command a hearing. They seemed to be having some success. Likewise the trade union leaders, who throughout the whole of the troubles showed great statesmanship and exercised considerable influence over their members, issued an appeal for peace and were remarkably successful in avoiding trouble. In the case of the shipyards this was particularly fortunate because they had a history of disturbance whenever there had been tension in the city.

But as Belfast seemed to retire from the headlines, eyes turned increasingly to Londonderry, where the traditional march of the Protestant Apprentice Boys of Derry was due to take place on August 12 to commemorate the 280th anniversary of the lifting of a siege imposed on the town by the Catholic King James II in 1689. History records that King James's troops were kept at bay for 15 weeks by 30,000 Protestants who crowded inside the walls of the city. The invading force seems to have been in no condition to undertake a serious attack and therefore encamped outside the walls in an attempt to starve the inhabitants into submission. Starvation grew inside the city, and reached a point where Colonel Robert Lundy, the Governor, seemed ready to negotiate. But the 30,000 Protestants remained adamant and tradition has it that 13 Protestant Apprentice Boys took affairs into their own hands and shut the

31

four great gates leading into the city to prevent negotiations from taking place. The Governor's name has since become synonymous with treachery and when I visited Londonderry, I had the name 'Lundy' flung at me by some Protestant extremists as I walked through the Protestant areas of the city. It was this victory of Protestants over Catholics which was to be commemorated on August 12, apparently regardless of the fact that the majority of the inhabitants are now Catholic.

The Governor of the Apprentice Boys, Dr Russel Abernethy, was the retired Medical Officer of Derry. He announced that despite the riots of the previous weekend, the march would go on: 'It would be a crime against the memory of the Apprentices and the continuity unbroken ever since, to interfere with the procession.' He said that hundreds of stewards would be present to marshal the expected crowd of 10,000 marchers and to keep the peace. It was his view that more trouble would be caused by an attempt to ban the march than by allowing it to go on. All this was inflammatory stuff for the Catholics in Londonderry and it was fanned when the Rev. Ian Paisley announced that he intended to lead a march through the Catholic town of Newry on the following Saturday, August 16. He said he would take as his text the words: 'From peace bought at the expense of truth, good Lord deliver us' – a fine statement but one that might be interpreted by some of his followers as an invitation to begin hostilities. His proposed march was gratuitously provocative and did not even have the excuse of celebrating some historic event.

The route followed by the marchers in Londonderry changes from year to year. By misfortune, in 1969 it was due to end high up on the city walls from which one can look down on the Catholic Bogside area huddled below. I discussed the march with Chichester-Clark and expressed my apprehensions about its taking place, especially in the light of a minute I had received from Harold Wilson, giving his view that the weekend violence in Belfast had shown manifestations out of all proportion to anything before. His minute expressed great doubts as to whether the march should be allowed to take place. I shared those doubts and consulted as many authorities as I could before raising the matter with Chichester-Clark.

His view was that a ban would probably be ineffective because the marchers would almost certainly go on to Londonderry. Even if the Government concentrated the police from the whole of Northern Ireland in Londonderry on that day, there would probably not be enough police to control the situation. Indeed some thought that a ban might even provoke an invasion of the Bogside area by some irresponsible Protestants who would feel that once again their Government – and I use the word 'their' advisedly because that was how they regarded it – had appeased the Catholics by banning a significant march. I did not have sufficient knowledge to reach a contrary conclusion. In any case, at that time the responsibility for law and order was still Chichester-Clark's, and in accordance with the Constitution the police were under the control of the Northern Ireland Government.

As the day approached, tension grew. Some were hard at work endeavouring to allay fears. John Hume, the young, able and hard-working Stormont Member for the Foyle Division of Londonderry whose constituency included the Bogside area, spent every day and much of the night working to damp down the increasing fears. On the whole, the Catholics seemed to believe that the Bogside was likely to be invaded whether the march went on or not and prepared themselves accordingly. The Derry Citizens Defence Association, which had been set up the previous month with the aim of protecting the area against either a Protestant or a police invasion, undoubtedly represented the genuine fears of many people. Some of the younger members of the community were quite eager to take part in any trouble that might start, and by the weekend they had erected barricades of paving stones, wooden shutters and other materials in a number of streets, leaving only narrow entrance points through which to pass. There was no doubt that they were substantially influenced by the events of the previous January and April, when a number of policemen had run through the Bogside using unnecessary violence, breaking windows and smashing glass in houses. There was a general determination, by no means confined to the young, that those events would not be repeated in August. In this atmosphere the attempts to lower the growing tension were doomed to failure, although even 'flower power' was tried when a group of teenagers of both religions went into the Protestant and Catholic areas on the Saturday, distributing among the elderly people what they called 'plants for peace', namely about two hundred pots of chrysanthemums. But this was not likely to offset the deep emotions that had been aroused.

While barricades were going up in the Catholic areas, street decorations of Union Jacks and bunting were being hung on houses in the Protestant areas. The Londonderry Commission, which had replaced the city council, tried to behave impartially by decorating Craigavon Bridge, over which the procession was due to pass, but leaving the Guildhall Square quite bare. Shopkeepers barricaded their windows and on the walls of the Bogside slogans were painted: 'No entry for Orangemen or the RUC.' Against this background the calls for self-discipline and peace put out by the Minister of Home Affairs, the Bishops and others sounded increasingly lame.

The celebrations began at midnight on Monday, August 11 when 'Roaring Meg', named after a Protestant siege gun used in the defence of the city in 1689, boomed out over the city. Bonfires were lit in the Protestant streets and Catholics and Protestants shouted abuse at each other. But the police pushed them apart and they gradually dispersed as the night wore on. When morning arrived it was a cold grey day and the march began peacefully enough with the drums, flutes and pipes leading the contingents, whose leaders wore a uniform of bowler hats, white cotton gloves and purple sashes, and carried umbrellas. Initially, indeed, the sectarian weapons seemed to be umbrellas for the Protestants and hurley sticks for the Catholics. The church bells played while the crowds stood silently watching the passing procession. No one could say it was a joyous parade like, for example, the annual Durham Miners' Gala – it was too solemn and tense. People seemed to feel that they were not so much celebrating past history as re-living it.

For nearly two hours the parade proceeded peacefully, but in the afternoon trouble broke out in Waterloo Place where a crowd of Catholic youths had assembled to jeer at the parade. They hurled stones at the marchers while the police, who showed considerable restraint in the early stages, did their best to prevent the situation from escalating. The marchers did not retaliate but the situation rapidly deteriorated when some Protestant bystanders, who were not part of the parade, picked up stones and hurled them back at the Catholic youths. Ivan Cooper, the local Stormont MP, who with

John Hume and others had been working hard to keep the peace, was hit in the face by a large stone and knocked unconscious.

As the day wore on, tempers on all sides worsened. The march itself came to an end and most of the visitors, who had travelled from many parts of the North, were quickly whisked away in 150 coaches, but enough remained for the troubles to continue. The tactics of the police seemed to be to drive the Catholic youths back into the Bogside and pen them there. Led by armoured cars and water cannon, they made a number of charges to the very border of the area, where they were met by volleys of stones and bottles hurled from behind the barricades. As the hatred grew and tempers flared, the bottles and stones became petrol bombs.

The police made no attempt to enter the Bogside but stood their ground, some of them hurling back at the rioters the bricks that were being thrown at them. I protested that their commanders should not have allowed this. It seemed to me to reduce the police to the same level as the rioters and anyway was not a tactic likely to succeed. Their visors and riot shields gave the police some protection; nevertheless one policeman was serioulsy wounded by a petrol bomb which exploded in his face and several others were carried away bleeding.

The Ulster Unionist Member for Londonderry at Westminster, Robin Chichester-Clark, the younger brother of the Prime Minister, went about on the Protestant side appealing to the crowd to disperse, but he had no more success than others. Members of the Press and television teams were jostled and abused.

During the evening, reinforcements for the police arrived from other parts of Northern Ireland bringing the total to 700, but as I had pointed out so often this was far too small a number to clear the streets. Indeed, attacks by the Catholic mobs grew even heavier and there seemed to have been no serious thinking about the tactics to be adopted by the police in these circumstances. This was a defect in the higher administration of the force.

Shortly before midnight on Tuesday, August 12, Chichester-Clark, who had cancelled a proposed visit to the United States, and Porter, the Minister of Home Affairs, met at police headquarters in Belfast. There was stalemate in the streets of Derry. The police, 82 of whom had been injured, had driven the Catholic youths back into the

Bogside but had got themselves into a position where they could neither advance nor withdraw. They had genuine fears that if they did not face the crowd where they stood, the mob would spill out of the Bogside and make for the Protestant area where they might well run riot. On the other side of the barricades, the Catholics felt that if they relaxed their guard and ceased to man the defences at the entrances to the Bogside, the police would sweep through the area and wreak vengeance on their homes in a repetition of the incidents in January and April.

So neither side could give way for neither side had any confidence in the other. It was a tragic situation. Each was convinced that the other meant violence and that to give way would be a disaster. The police made one more effort to subdue and disperse the crowd just before midnight. A police armoured vehicle moved forward to the edge of the barricades and for the first time fired canisters of tear gas into the crowd. This had an immediate but only temporary effect. Initially the crowds dispersed coughing and weeping from the effects of the gas, but as these wore off they reassembled behind the barricades which remained intact throughout the following two days.

During the early hours of Wednesday morning, the Bogside was lit by the flames of buildings that had been set on fire, including a bakery, the local Court House, factories and even private houses. The police held on grimly in their lines in front of the barricades, even though administrative incompetence left the men on the ground largely without refreshment and without reinforcements. The confrontation settled down to almost a ritual performance: the mob threw petrol bombs and stones sporadically and the police responded with volleys of CS gas which drifted to and fro between the lines choking rioters and police indiscriminately.

The centre of the battle became a ten-storey block of flats in the Bogside on the top of which the Republican flag was hoisted. The roof provided a perfect vantage point from which rioters hurled their bombs and stones on the policemen below. It was heart-rending to see on television children of nine and ten years of age filling crates of milk bottles with petrol stolen from a post office depot and stuffing rags into the mouths of the bottles to make lethal petrol bombs. It was during Wednesday that the dramatic picture was taken of Bernadette Devlin apparently smashing a huge paving stone to provide rocks to hurl. This was flashed around the world together with derogatory editorial comments.

By nightfall on Wednesday, the police were dog-tired and unable to hold the exposed position they had taken up. They were ordered to retreat some two hundred yards and then, as though they were an advancing army, the rioters immediately occupied the ground that the police had abandoned and set to work to build another huge barricade at the new limit of their territory.

One oddity of the situation, which despite my later questioning was never satisfactorily explained, was why the police apparently made no attempt to gain control by tackling the rioters from the rear, for throughout the battle there were other entrances to the Bogside that remained unguarded. I never could find out whether the police command considered it and ruled it out, whether the men were too tired, or whether the command itself was too static. I find it difficult to believe that a properly organized and well-led police force would have allowed a riot to degenerate into stalemate without taking some fresh initiatives. Indeed, on Thursday night after the Army had taken over they heard that some Protestant activists were actually planning to approach the Bogside from the rear. They stepped in to prevent this, but if the Protestants could envisage such a raid it is hard to know why the police did not. Of course it would have meant another 'invasion' of the Bogside, but it could hardly have made matters any worse, and might conceivably have broken up the rioters.

The longer the situation went on, the less room there was for compromise between the people of the Bogside and the RUC. On Wednesday evening, the Derry Citizens Defence Association announced that they were all set for a long confrontation and ready to hold the barricades indefinitely. There would be no peace, they said, until the RUC pulled out and Stormont was abolished. That was uncompromising enough. The police, on the other hand, while unable to take the initiative, felt they could not withdraw without a complete and final loss of authority. I was told on Wednesday evening that the Ulster Unionist Government, meeting in continuing and anxious session, had no other proposal to make than to use the B-Specials. They did so, but they had the wisdom to confine their activities to the Protestant part of Londonderry, thus enabling a

few more policemen to be released to confront the Bogside barricades. As the day drew on, with reports of a constantly deteriorating
situation, it seemed only too evident that the moment was coming
when, as *The Times* put it: 'Stormont will have failed and it will be
the turn of Westminster to renew its acquaintance with the Irish
Question – a prospect that any sensible politician must pray he will
be spared.'

The understanding between the Northern Ireland Government
and ourselves had been limited up to then to providing British
troops for the static defence of key installations in remote areas.
It was understood and agreed by them that before their Inspector-
General of Constabulary called on British troops for assistance
under the Common Law, the Northern Ireland Government would
make a direct approach through their Prime Minister to me.
Lord Stonham, who was acting as Minister in charge of the Home
Office at this time, told me it was his view, as well as that of Philip
Allen, that that moment was practically upon us.

It so happened that Mr Maudling, the Deputy Leader of the
Opposition, had asked to see Lord Stonham on Wednesday afternoon, August 13, and Lord Stonham took the opportunity to make
this view known to him, together with a clear statement that, in
these circumstances, and after taking advice from General Freeland,
the General Officer Commanding, the British Government would be
fully prepared to authorize him to give all help that was necessary
to protect life and property.

Having received this assessment, I telephoned Harold Wilson in
the Scillies, and told him the position. The Prime Minister naturally
wanted to be informed at first hand before such a serious step was
agreed to and he suggested that I should fly to Culdrose Royal Naval
Air Station in Cornwall the next day, Thursday, and he would meet
me there having come by helicopter from the Scillies. Accordingly we
made stand-by arrangements and left a final decision on whether
we should meet until early on Thursday morning.

When I arrived back in London at 11 p.m. on Wednesday night
I was met at my home by an anxious Private Secretary with a
message that I should go immediately to the Home Office. There I
found officials in a state of some alarm because reports were coming
in of a broadcast by Mr Jack Lynch, the Prime Minister of the

Republic, made earlier that evening. As usual on such occasions, we could not get hold of an exact text and had to rely on the reports on the news agency tape. But Tom McCaffery, the extremely resourceful and well informed chief information officer at the Home Office, used his contacts to get fuller information. What we learnt in no way comforted us.

Lynch said in his broadcast that Stormont was no longer in control of the situation and that the RUC could not be accepted as an impartial police force. He also went on to say that the employment of British troops to restore order would not be acceptable either, and further, that the Irish Government could not stand by and see innocent people injured. He had therefore directed the Irish Army to open field hospitals in Donegal and at other points along the border so that those who had been injured in the rioting could be treated in the South. He had also instructed the Irish permanent representative at the United Nations to see U Thant, the Secretary-General, and inform him that the Republic of Ireland had officially requested Britain to ask the UN to despatch a peace-keeping force urgently to the border.

When I heard this, late at night, it really seemed to be putting the fat in the fire. Following Lynch's statement, and a call by the Civil Rights Association for diversionary demonstrations, riots and disturbances took place on a wider scale throughout the province that night than at any time since the civil war of 1921-2.

As the small group of officials waited with me at the Home Office in the early hours of the morning stories were coming in of disturbances in Belfast, Armagh, Dungannon, Lurgan, Newry, Dungiven and Enniskillen. It is possible, of course, that these were a natural reaction to events in Londonderry during the previous forty-eight hours, but we had no way of telling the cause or of assessing the seriousness of these outbreaks from the scanty messages as they arrived. We had to consider the possibility that within the next twenty-four hours we might face both civil war in the North and an invasion from the South. I frankly could not believe that the second was possible.

I had first met Lynch at the annual conferences of the International Monetary Fund whilst he was Minister of Finance and I was Chancellor of the Exchequer. From talking to him I believed him to be a cool, level-headed person, not easily swept off his feet. I have not subsequently changed my view. I did not really believe that he would involve the South in an invasion of the North; nevertheless, the talk of opening hospitals on the border might conceivably be a blind for further troop movements, and it would have been imprudent to have ignored it. So our talks at the Home Office took an even more serious turn and we discussed the action that would have to be taken in the event of various unlikely contingencies, including the disposition of British troops on the border.

In time the real attitude of Mr Lynch and his Government became much clearer. Subsequent statements of his rapidly confirmed that he adhered without qualification to the ultimate aim of a united Ireland which is proclaimed in Article 2 of the Constitution of the Republic: 'The National Territory consists of the whole Island of Ireland, its islands and the territorial seas.' But he also made clear that he did not believe that unity could be enforced, and indeed he knows that it cannot. Nevertheless, that night he had to respond to some of the hard liners in his own Government, such as Neil Blaney, the Agriculture Minister, who represented the border county of Donegal and wanted to see some action. Lynch had to be seen to be taking some action. In addition to calling for a United Nations force, he also announced that he was sending Irish Army medical units to the Border, backed, we understood, by a logistical support force of the 6th Battalion Athlone and the 1st Battalion Galway Regiments. In taking this step, Lynch almost overstepped the mark with Irish opinion in the Republic. The people were deeply concerned about the North and they wanted their Government to express their concern in a vigorous and forceful way, but they certainly did not want a confrontation between the Irish troops and the British Army. However, we were not to know all this at the time and Lynch's speech undoubtedly increased tension and anxiety among the Protestants in the North.

Chichester-Clark fired off an immediate indignant reply and at the same time decided to mobilize the 8000 B-Specials and to issue their officers with revolvers. They were ordered to report to their nearest police stations to carry out riot patrol duties. This was not cleared with the British Government beforehand and indeed there was no direct charge upon Chichester-Clark to do so, for his Government was still in charge of security in the North. Nevertheless, there had been an understanding between the British Government and the Northern Ireland Government that the 600 members of the B-Specials who had been mobilized earlier would only be used to guard static posts and would not be used for riot control. The news of the mobilization of this exclusively Protestant force spread quickly and increased tension at a most inopportune moment.

That was the situation on the morning of August 14 when I set off early from Gatwick Airport to meet the Prime Minister at Culdrose. By this time my mind was made up that despite the quicksands of Irish politics we would have to send in British troops, for the Northern Ireland Government could hardly claim to be in control of the situation.

Before the Cabinet had broken up for the summer recess they had agreed to leave operational decisions in the hands of the Prime Minister, the Foreign Secretary, Michael Stewart, the Defence Secretary, Denis Healey and myself, assuming that the Cabinet itself could not be called together. Michael Stewart was on holiday in Europe and Denis Healey was recovering from a minor operation, so the responsibility devolved upon Harold Wilson and myself. Although I respected the judgement of my colleagues on this matter, on the whole I find decisions are fastest when the fewest people are consulted. I was not altogether unhappy, therefore, that it would fall to Harold Wilson and me to reach the fateful decision.

As we flew over Devon, we were told that a sea fret in Cornwall would prevent us landing in Culdrose, so we flew on to St Mawgan RAF Station. Together with the officials who accompanied me, I brought the Prime Minister up to date on the situation and in his usual manner he asked a number of detailed and factual questions, some of which sent officials scurrying for answers. We did not have a map of Northern Ireland with us, so when at one point Wilson wanted to know how far somewhere was from somewhere else the Group Captain hurried off and came back with a small atlas which we all pored over. Harold Wilson was in full agreement with the measures to be taken, so our discussion on the principle of intervention did not take very long. By mid-afternoon we were able to meet the Press for an informal interview, after which he flew back to the Scillies and I returned to London.

We had not been in the air for more than ten minutes when the navigator came into the cabin with a pencilled message scribbled on a signal pad. It had been relayed from the Home Office and tersely informed us that an official request for the use of troops had been made by the Northern Ireland Government. I immediately scribbled 'Permission granted' on the signal pad and handed it back to the navigator. He then said that I could speak to the Home Office direct if I wished and he could connect me via Lyneham airfield in Wiltshire. For some minutes we flew on without a connection being established and eventually Lyneham was almost directly underneath us. Because of some technical trouble, I did not in the end speak to them and I was later told that the message to the Home Office giving consent had eventually to be relayed via Gibraltar!

A few minutes later, General Freeland's troops began to relieve the police in the Bogside amid loud jubilation from the inhabitants. Four hundred troops of the 1st Battalion Prince of Wales Own Yorkshire Regiment under the Command of Lieut.-Colonel W. Todd were the first to move, one company literally turning round in mid-air while being flown back to England as part of the normal changeover. Their immediate orders were to relieve the exhausted police and to prevent riots breaking out in the centre of Londonderry. In the initial stages they were joined by a large number of B-Specials armed with rifles. Colonel Todd and some of his officers, who had reconnoitred the territory earlier in plain clothes, set up road blocks at all entrances to Londonderry to prevent cars moving in, and sought out the Derry Citizens Defence Association. Its leaders were in such a jubilant mood that they were ready to overlook the fact that it was British troops who were investing the Bogside. On any other occasion they would have taken the most violent exception to them. However, they soon agreed to a three-point plan under which the B-Specials were to be withdrawn, the RUC were to resume normal police duties, while the defence association would try to calm down the crowds. In contrast to the fever heat of the previous days, the temperature of the area quickly fell. The B-Specials withdrew from the Bogside perimeter to patrol Protestant areas, but there was no immediate resumption of normal RUC patrols, for truth to tell they had not carried out normal duties in the Bogside for some years.

When I got back to the Home Office I was informed that earlier in the afternoon Sir Harold Black, the Secretary to the Northern Ireland Cabinet, had telephoned to say that Anthony Peacocke, the Inspector-General, feared that the police would be unable to contain the Bogside for much longer and that if troops were not made available the police would be compelled to retreat from their position in front of the barricades to Victoria Police Station. They feared that the centre of the city would then be invaded by a riotous mob with the prospect of looting, arson, injury to persons and extensive damage to property. An hour and a half later Black had telephoned again to say that the Inspector-General was at that moment formally asking for the assistance of troops, and that was the message I received in the air.

It seemed to me essential that the British Government should make two things clear: first, it should be emphasized that the troops would act impartially in restoring law and order, for the Catholic population was undoubtedly in a state of very great fear; and second, in order to calm the Protestants, we should reaffirm that the arrival of British troops would in no way weaken the pledge that had been given that Northern Ireland would not cease to be part of the United Kingdom without the consent of the Parliament of Northern Ireland. I therefore issued a statement in the following terms:

'The Government of Northern Ireland has informed the United Kingdom Government that as a result of the severe and prolonged rioting in Londonderry it has no alternative but to ask for the assistance of the troops at present stationed in Northern Ireland to prevent a breakdown of law and order.

'After three days and two nights of continuous duty the Royal Ulster Constabulary find it necessary to fall back on their police stations, thus exposing the citizens of Londonderry to the prospect of looting and a danger to life.

'The United Kingdom Government has received assessments of the situation from the Northern Ireland Government and the GOC Northern Ireland, and has agreed to this request in order to restore order in Londonderry with the greatest possible speed.

'The GOC Northern Ireland has been instructed to take all the necessary steps, acting impartially between citizen and citizen to restore law and order.

'Troops will be withdrawn as soon as this is accomplished. This is a limited operation and during it the troops will remain in direct and exclusive control of the GOC, who will continue to be responsible to the United Kingdom Government.

'The Ireland Act, 1949, affirms that neither Northern Ireland nor any part of it will in any event cease to be part of the United Kingdom without the consent of the Parliament of Northern Ireland, and the United Kingdom Government reaffirms the pledges previously given that this will remain the position so long as the people of Northern Ireland wish.

'The United Kingdom Government has ultimate responsibility for the protection of those who live in Northern Ireland when, as on this occasion, a breakdown of law and order has occurred.'

4

It may be thought strange that these reassurances were necessary. But enough Protestants were in the ugly and aggressive mood to wreak serious destruction and damage on the minority if they suspected Mr Lynch's call might be listened to by the British Government, while the Catholic minority genuinely feared attack by the Protestants and some were desperate enough to go on the offensive themselves in what might be termed a pre-emptive strike. Our hope was that the mere presence of British troops would be enough to restrain both sides without the soldiers having to fire a shot, and would also be sufficient to end the mob rule that existed in parts of the province. We also made clear that although troops were going to the aid of the civil power in Northern Ireland, the ultimate chain of command lay through the GOC to the Secretary of State for Defence in London and thence to the Cabinet.

This could have been a constitutional cat's cradle in that although the troops were not taking their orders from the Northern Ireland Government, they were nevertheless embroiled in a situation which was the responsibility of that Government. O'Neill had foreseen this clearly when he was Prime Minister and had recognized that the relationship between the Government at Westminster and the Government of Northern Ireland would be altered from the moment that the first British soldiers went on to the streets. It was obvious that the Westminster Government would assume a close interest both in the executive actions of the Northern Ireland Government and in their general policy, if British troops were to be at the receiving end of disagreements on that policy. So Great Britain was inexorably drawn back into the Irish Question, into a heady brew made up of pleas for specified rights for the minority coupled with the desire to upset the settlement of 1921 by others, and offset by

45

the enraged response of many 'Loyalists' who felt that 'their' police had been defied and humiliated.

There was also a strong feeling among the extreme Protestants that the minority was receiving much too favourable attention from the world Press.

Against this background, the Stormont Parliament held an emergency session and Chichester-Clark made an attack on Lynch. He said: 'We must and we will treat the Government who seeks to wound us in our darkest hour as an unfriendly and implacable Government, determined to overthrow by any means the State which enjoys the support of a majority of our electorate.' He went on to say that a conspiracy existed in which hooligans were being 'manipulated and encouraged by those who sought to discredit and overthrow this Government'. Although there was some truth in what he said, as a total explanation of the near civil war it was woefully incomplete. The Northern Ireland Prime Minister seemed to revert to the traditional historic attitude in the dispute about the border as though this were the only point at issue. But of course in public on many other occasions, as well as in private, he acknowledged the need for reforms in the treatment of the minority.

For their part, the Catholics were determined to have their revenge by humiliating the Protestant Ulster Unionist Government that had ruled over them for fifty years. At the Bogside they succeeded. My own impression of those early days is that elements such as the IRA played only a minor part in the developing events. Indeed, it was not until four days later that the Chief of Staff of the IRA, Cathal Goulding, issued a statement saying that armoured units had been sent North, and warning the British troops that while the IRA had no quarrel with them as individuals, they could be in a perilous situation if they were used to suppress the legitimate demands of the minority. The IRA said that they had 'used their all too limited resources' in Belfast, urged the Dublin Government to employ the Irish Army to defend the people of the North, and ended by calling on Britain to get out of the country.

Lynch replied sharply to this statement, saying that no group had any authority to speak or act for the Irish people except the lawful and properly elected Government. He went on to condemn the 'wanton destruction to property and the lawless behaviour by a small minority' which had been taking place in Dublin during the past week. 'This irresponsible behaviour and criminal conduct can do nothing to help our brethren in the Six Counties,' he said. There was no doubt that this statement reflected the genuine anger felt in Dublin at the IRA statement. They were regarded as a small body who had little influence on what had taken place in the North and who, in trying to capitalize on those events, were playing into the hands of the Northern extremists. All the reports that I received both before and during this time showed that there was a sizeable generation gap between various elements in the IRA and that the organization was split into small splinter groups with different conceptions of their role. As Tim Pat Coogan wrote in his book, *The I.R.A.*: 'It exists as a traditional rather than a cohesive movement.'

In 1969 the IRA was only a pale shadow of a movement which had once boasted upwards of 30,000 members. The divisions in its depleted ranks came to a head in 1962 when the organization called off its six year campaign of resistance to British occupation, dumped its arms and withdrew its full-time active service volunteers. It admitted then that the abandonment of its policies had been caused by lack of public support. Nevertheless, some elements still clung to their traditional methods and robbed banks to get funds and burned down German-owned farm houses to express their nationalism. Official IRA policy became more openly political during the years before 1969 and veered strongly to the extreme left. Members of the IRA undoubtedly played a part in the civil rights movement but it would be overestimating their importance to assume that they controlled it. Among the guiding spirits of the civil rights movement were men like Gerry Fitt, Ivan Cooper and John Hume, and it was under their leadership, among others, that the movement caught the sympathy and attention of the world by skilfully fostering such legitimate demands as one man one vote in local elections, no discrimination in the allocation of local authority houses, no discrimination by the police, and so on. The IRA had few members in August 1968 and it was not until later that it reorganized and mobilized. I believe that if events had not gone so tragically wrong in the summer of 1970, the IRA might have broken fresh ground with an entirely new policy of recognizing Stormont and of working through the civil rights association and similar organizations. This may sound a bold claim, but I believe we were within a touch of this happening. In any case, as we have seen, the IRA itself has since split and it was the Provisional Army Council – the Provos – and not the official IRA who favoured the mounting of a campaign of guerilla war against the British Army. The Provos gained the ascendancy, but they did so only by capturing the support of the majority of the Catholic population after insensitive British handling had disenchanted it. If other political courses had been followed in 1970 and 1971, it is possible that the official IRA would have kept their hold and the Provisionals would never have gained the the ground they did.

Meanwhile, on that evening of August 14, when all our eyes were focused on the reception that the British troops were getting in Londonderry, trouble was breaking out once more in Belfast. The scene was confused, but as the reports came in the prevailing impression left on me was that again it was the extreme Protestants who were the instigators of the violence. During the day I had had a telephone conversation with Gerry Fitt, who rang me to say that he and his wife had both been threatened with physical violence, if not worse, after nightfall and that many other Catholics were also living in fear of what would happen. It was my view that the Protestants were enraged by the Catholics' successful defiance of the RUC in Londonderry, the reports of Lynch's speech, and the accounts of field hospitals being set up near the border.

The fuse may have been slower to ignite in Belfast, but once it had been touched off the explosion was devastating. Nor was this the only trouble spot. Shots were fired in Omagh, and in Armagh the riots claimed their first victim when John Gallagher, a Catholic, was shot dead. There were numerous clashes between Catholics and Protestants. B-Specials made baton charges against Catholic mobs and factories were set on fire and gutted. But it was in Belfast on the night of the 14th that the trouble was most serious. As I sat in the Home Office reports came in of Sten guns being used, bombs being thrown, snipers situated on high buildings and of police armoured cars using Browning machine-guns. The situation grew worse, and three men and a boy aged nine were killed and three policemen and many civilians wounded during the night. Large gangs of Protestants gathered in Newtownards and Shankill Road, and other gangs of Catholic youths erected barricades across streets where they ran into Protestant areas, to prevent the feared invasion by the Protestants and also to stop the police from entering. At one stage, after charges in which the Catholics had been driven back, a number of so-called Protestants swept down the road after them, setting fire to buildings and houses as they went. Then I was told that the B-Specials, who by this time had been armed by the Ulster Unionist Government, were out in force. As a wholly Protestant force they were subjected to a fusillade of missiles from the Catholics. The Protestants supporting the B-Specials replied in kind, and within a few hours of nightfall the Falls Road district was turned into a senseless scene of riot and destruction with windows smashed, cars overturned, paving stones prised up to be used both as barricades and weapons, petrol bombs being thrown, and public houses set on fire.

Gerry Fitt telephoned again and said that only British troops could restore calm in Belfast. There was no doubt that his apprehensions were genuine but I could not forbear to remind him that Lynch had said that British troops would be unwelcome. What was his opinion? Fitt was emphatic that the Catholic minority in Belfast would not take that view: only British troops could save them from the wrath of the Protestants and he urged that they should be brought in at once.

During the next day, August 15, I had two long conversations with Chichester-Clark. I told him of my decision to send two senior police officers to act as observers and keep me informed. They were Robert Mark, Deputy Commissioner of the Metropolitan Police, who has since become the Commissioner, and Douglas Osmond, the Chief Constable of Hampshire, both outstanding policemen. I also said I thought we should meet to discuss what action and policy changes the Ulster Government would need to undertake. Chichester-Clark did not actually demur but neither did he seem over-keen; he said that he needed to be on the spot while the situation was so serious, and would have to wait and see whether it improved. He sounded almost hopeful, despite the shooting during the night, because the shipyard workers at Harland and Wolff, who were overwhelmingly Protestant, were meeting at midday to press for an end to violence. But at 12.25 a formal request came from the

Northern Ireland Government for further troops for use in Belfast.
I gave immediate approval.

During these few days while Denis Healey was undergoing a minor
operation, Roy Hattersley was in charge at the Ministry of Defence.
I found him always unruffled, extremely clear and firm, and helpful
in all that he did. I was very grateful to him.

When I spoke to Chichester-Clark again that afternoon I asked
him, in view of the fact that he had deployed the B-Specials on his
own responsibility, what his intentions were for the future. He
seemed to agree that their attempts to control the crowds and the
rioters the previous night had increased rather than subdued the
troubles, and said that henceforth they would be kept in reserve at
police stations and used for patrolling in Protestant areas only. He
said he had considered closing the border in the light of Lynch's
statement and I replied that such a step would be ineffective. There
were barely enough troops available for riot control in the areas
immediately affected and the closure would therefore be only a
gesture. As we were speaking, the 2nd Battalion The Queen's Regiment was moving towards Belfast together with the 1st Battalion
The Royal Regiment of Wales. At the same time the Ministry of
Defence had given orders for 600 men from the 3rd Battalion Light
Infantry to fly from Lyneham in Wiltshire, and the 1st Battalion
Royal Green Jackets at Tidworth, Hampshire, was recalled from
leave and put on stand-by. A day or two later, the 1st Battalion
The Royal Hampshire Regiment was also recalled from leave. The
17/21 Lancers, an armoured car regiment, was stationed in Northern
Ireland at the time, but was depleted by having two squadrons overseas in Libya and Cyprus. Altogether 4000 soldiers were available
at the beginning of the troubles and this was stepped up to 6000
within a week. As the whole strength of the RUC was no more than
3000, this reinforcement trebled the total numbers available, and as
the Army did not work on a shift system the effective increase was
even bigger, in the short run.

General Sir Ian Freeland, the GOC Northern Ireland, had been
in Northern Ireland for only a few weeks but he proved to be a
tower of strength. His manner was both authoritative and relaxed,
and conveyed the correct impression of a man who knew what
needed to be done and would do it. His very appearance on the

TV screens was a reassurance, and I soon found we had a man of understanding and decision.

The 500 troops who entered Belfast in the early evening of Friday, August 15, threw a cordon between the warring Catholic and Protestant factions. In the areas that they occupied there was comparative calm, but in other areas, even those close by where the police were trying to control the situation, rioting was fierce, and the police station in Tennent Street was fired at and attacked by petrol bombs.

There was small arms and machine-gun fire during the night. A number of policemen and civilians were shot and injured, and one British soldier was slightly wounded. Rows of houses were deliberately set on fire in Cupar Street, Bombay Street and Kashmir Street, but the shooting was so fierce that the firemen were unable to get to the blaze. In areas where the soldiers were patrolling, people came out from behind the barricades and tea and biscuits were passed to them with smiles and expressions of welcome. Nevertheless, only a short distance away, double-decker buses were being hi-jacked to make barricades. It was indeed a confused situation.

There was a lot of other activity during the day. Mr Heath and Mr Thorpe were both away – Heath somewhere off the south-west coast of Ireland sailing in the Fastnet race – so I asked Maudling, acting Leader of the Opposition, to see me, and, separately, Eric Lubbock of the Liberal Party. I gave them both as much information as I could about the situation and our general intentions. Neither of them disagreed with what we were doing, nor with the decision to send in troops.

While I was seeing them, Dr Patrick Hillery, Minister of External Affairs in the Republic, who had seen the Foreign Secretary a fortnight earlier, arrived in London to see Lord Chalfont, Minister of State at the Foreign Office. Lord Stonham, Minister of State at the Home Office, went across to the Foreign Office to join in the discussions. Hillery asked that a peace-keeping force of British and Irish troops should be sent to the North, and called for the abolition of the B-Specials. He told the Press afterwards that he had received what he called 'a courteous brush-off'.

Saturday, August 16, the day after troops had gone into Belfast, was a full working day from 10 a.m. to midnight. A changing group of people, Home Office officials, Ministry of Defence, and Cabinet Office secretariat, were in almost continuous session in my room at the Home Office, coming and going as they needed to while we took decisions about the changing situation. The most important task during the day was to try to give effect to Chichester-Clark's promise to take the B-Specials off the streets and riot control duties, so I spent some time discussing with Roy Hattersley and his officials my urgent request to make more troops available who could be used instead.

Late on Saturday afternoon I received a request from the Northern Ireland Government that Royal Engineers should be sent immediately to blow up minor roads between the North and the South in order to make it easier to control cross-border traffic. The Foreign and Commonwealth Office and the Ministry of Defence were both ready to agree, but no one could give me any evidence that what was passing over the border would seriously worsen the position in Londonderry or Belfast. As the cratering of the roads would worsen relations with the Republic without doing anything very effective to ease the situation in Northern Ireland, I could not conclude that it would help my policy of cooling the situation.

A day or so later, Sir Andrew Gilchrist, our Ambassador in Dublin, reported that the Irish Government intended to seek a debate on the situation in the Security Council. This reinforced my opposition to blowing up the roads – the issue was still dragging on – because our answer to the Security Council would be that Northern Ireland was a domestic issue. I thought that our position might be weakened if the Irish Government could say that the roads across the border were being blown up, and that the problem was therefore something more than a domestic issue. In the end, no more was heard of the matter and it was dropped for the time being.

The initiative taken by the Republic of Ireland at the United Nations ultimately worked out to the satisfaction of both sides. If the UN's constitution had been strictly interpreted, Hillery could have been prevented from asking the Security Council to put his Government's request for a United Nations force on the agenda, on the grounds that it was a domestic matter, and therefore outside the UN's jurisdiction. But Lord Caradon, who was our chief permanent representation at the UN, handled the matter very wisely. 'As a matter of courtesy', he said, Britain would agree to Hillery being granted a hearing. The Irish Minister responded with a moderately phrased speech. He said that the presence of British troops was unacceptable because they signified the perpetuation of partition. The police force in Northern Ireland was mistrusted and detested and was suppressing a civil rights movement which was aiming at ending discrimination against the Catholic minority. He suggested that a United Nations peace-keeping force would be the best means of defusing a dangerous situation and preventing 'the virtual collapse of the machinery of law and order'. As soon as he finished, the Zambian delegate proposed that the debate should be adjourned.

This move was the result of extensive consultations among the member states before the meeting on the best way of hearing the Irish appeal without officially taking it up. The Soviet and Spanish, as well as some Afro-Asian, delegates were anxious that the appeal should be heard. It would then have been within Britain's rights to have insisted on a vote being taken on the adjournment motion, and there is no doubt that we could have raised sufficient votes to avoid having the matter inscribed on the agenda. But, wisely again, Lord Caradon did not press a vote. He said he understood that an adjournment motion meant that the Security Council did not accept, and would not proceed with, the item. Hillery said afterwards that he knew there was no prospect of a UN peace-keeping force. But Lord Caradon's approach avoided giving him a personal rebuff while adhering firmly to the British position, and Lynch was able to show his fellow countrymen that he had taken the matter to the Security Council and done as much as he could.

Fortunately, while the troubles in Belfast were at their height, Londonderry remained quiet. Nevertheless we never regarded it as being more than a lull. Within twenty-four hours of the troops going in it was apparent that it would be difficult to withdraw them without recreating the very conditions they had been sent in to end. Obviously major political changes would have to be made.

5

Seen from the Home Office two things were becoming clear. First, the security arrangements were in a mess, for both the RUC and the Army operated independently and the mobilization of the B-Specials was a handicap in creating an acceptable peace force. Both Harold Wilson and Denis Healey pressed for the issue to be cleared up. Of even greater long-term importance was the need to meet the legitimate civil rights demands of the minority without enraging still further the mob element among the extreme Protestants which had already done enough damage. A new contract was needed between the two communities, and Harold Wilson decided to break his short holiday and call a conference at Downing Street to see if a fresh start could be made.

The first thing we had to do was to get Chichester-Clark to London, and the date of the meeting was finally set for Tuesday, August 19. When I telephoned him the night before he sounded pretty glum. He too had now reached the conclusion that public confidence in the police had ebbed away and that an inquiry into the RUC was needed. He had told Anthony Peacocke, the Inspector-General, of this and Peacocke had reacted unfavourably. Chichester-Clark said he was afraid that Peacocke might resign and that if he did it would be followed by mass resignations from the force. At that moment Jack Andrews, the Deputy Prime Minister, was touring police stations trying to rally morale, which was very low, and make the RUC feel that not all the world was against them. I told Chichester-Clark that Robert Mark and Douglas Osmond, the two police officers I had sent over as observers, had reported that the top leadership of the RUC was poor and that Peacocke would have to be replaced.

I asked Chichester-Clark what his attitude would be to the

Cameron Report, a draft of which had just come into our hands and was due from the printers. It dealt with the causes and nature of the civil disturbances in the province between October 1968 and January 1969 and was in parts highly critical of the Unionist Government. I said I thought it would be right to say that a lot had happened since then and that to some extent what Cameron said had been overtaken by events. We agreed to discuss it again later.

I then raised the question of the pirate radios, which had been worrying me for two or three days. A number had sprung up in Belfast and I had had complaints that they were exacerbating the situation by fanning the flames of sectarian bitterness. I was being asked if it was possible to stop them. John Stonehouse, the Postmaster General, had received a report from Belfast saying that it was technically possible but that it was for me to decide whether it was politically desirable. The argument dragged on for some time before we took action to jam them.

We usually began our conversations, incidentally, with a discussion about the harvest: how was he getting on? Well, his barley was three weeks behind mine. And what were the yields like? Well, his were pretty good and mine, perhaps, were a bit lighter. And how were the cattle, and how were the market prices going? This was my rather obvious way of taking the tension out of the situation, by getting him on familiar territory. He was most at home when he was at Castledawson, a country house in Co. Londonderry with 400 acres where he and his wife were working farmers. He used to retire there as often as he could and had to be prised out to come to Belfast. I think the Home Office used to laugh at these bucolic telephone conversations of ours, but they were a very useful way of getting Chichester-Clark to relax before we got down to business.

On the morning of the 19th, the day of the Downing Street conference, I took Douglas Osmond, who was the Chief Constable of Hampshire, to see the Prime Minister because I wanted the PM to understand how well-founded my anxieties were about the RUC. Osmond and Robert Mark had been in Northern Ireland since the 16th and some of their findings were very disturbing indeed. Their first criticism was that the Minister of Home Affairs seemed totally dependent on the Inspector-General. He was the Minister's sole source of intelligence and professional advice, and the Minister seemed to take second place to him. They said the Inspector-General's office seemed to be an informal meeting place for any Minister or civil servant who cared to drop in, and he clearly held a position of very great authority. They thought this a great weakness, and were really rather horrified by it. They said that Peacocke's approach was sensational and that it was coupled with a very poor intelligence network. After an abortive attempt to blow up Armagh police station he had deployed three armoured columns to patrol the border, apparently in the belief that this was the right response. As to the Deputy Inspector-General, Graham Shillington, they said he was a rational, unemotional, likeable person. The Commissioner for Belfast, Harold Wolseley, was desperately tired, a gentle and depressed man. In Londonderry, it was their view that the wrong men were in command. The County Inspector, who had been promoted in July, was weak and ineffectual. He had been overwhelmed by the County Inspector in charge of traffic control, who was pompous, dogmatic and self-important. Both were quite unsuited to handle the situation that had arisen. However, there was a useful District Inspector there, and some excellent middle rank officers.

'The men feel they have done their best,' Mark and Osmond reported, 'and they are bewildered and angry at the reaction of the Press and the public. The ordinary policeman feels an injustice has been done to him. They have all been on duty for long periods but there has been no real organization by the top-level command for proper reliefs or even for such ordinary domestic details as hot meals at night. All this should have been done and would have been done in any equivalent demonstration in Britain.' Indeed, we had experience of this during the Grosvenor Square demonstration in October 1968 when the Metropolitan Police took over the basement behind the US Embassy and used it as a canteen. On that occasion the men in the front rank who bore the brunt of the charges were withdrawn at intervals, went into the canteen and had hot drinks, and then went back into the front line. Sir John Waldron, the Commissioner, who was there all day, rightly did not want me in the Square making his task more difficult. So I had to watch the events of the afternoon on a television set in my room in the Home

Office. However, I went to the Square as soon as I could overcome his discouragement and convinced myself that the police as a whole had been properly looked after, although, even so, a few units from the suburbs were overlooked. But in general the police response to that massive demonstration was organized superbly. They allowed the demonstration to go on and yet basically kept control of it. I thought of Grosvenor Square many times during those days in August 1969.

Mark and Osmond were very critical of the fact that police stations were bolted and barred. This was a hangover from the IRA menace, which they did not believe was serious at that time, and seemed to be the traditional reaction to any new situation. The police, they said, were on the defensive. Sentries had been armed with machine-guns at the stations; there were large numbers of men sitting around in poor accommodation waiting for something to happen. And they described how they went in to one country police station which was shuttered, bolted and barred – nothing could be seen except the smiling Irish afternoon – and they banged on the shutters and eventually an apprehensive man put his head round the door and they said, 'Look, we happen to be English policemen. Can we come and see what you're doing?' They found the station covered in litter and cigarette stubs and the vehicles and other equipment dirty. The men were just sitting there waiting for a non-existent attack to be made on them. Mark and Osmond went back there three or four days later and found things in exactly the same disorganized and dirty state.

They blamed the higher command for this. The public could not get near some stations, they said, because they were so heavily guarded. No one could get near the headquarters of the Londonderry district because there were armed sentries to be seen even in full daylight, although conditions immediately outside the station were apparently normal. They said the force was obsessed with the belief that the rioting was the result of a deep IRA plot. The RUC had little information about the civil rights movement, the Paisleyites or the Ulster Protestant Volunteers, and no source of intelligence at all inside the Bogside. Long before August 1969 there had been little or no law enforcement system inside the Bogside. Crimes and assaults went unreported and uninvestigated: no one in the area would think of invoking police assistance. There was a similar situation in the no-go areas of Belfast. It was, Mark and Osmond said, a complete defeat for the force.

This was not all entirely new to us, but it was the first time it had been so clearly reported, and it illustrated one of the weaknesses of the constitutional relationship between Britain and Northern Ireland. This fundamental antipathy between the police and a substantial section of the population had persisted for years within the United Kingdom, yet no UK Minister had any responsibility, or indeed opportunity, to find out what was going on. And even if he had found out, so long as the relationship remained as it was and so long as the tension remained below the surface and did not come out into the open and become a subject of public comment, there was little any UK Minister could have done even if he had wanted to stir up such a hornet's nest.

Mark and Osmond said the police were in no way presented to the public as a safeguard or sign of stability. 'They are a force apart,' was how they put it. There was no real system for handling complaints against the police, who seemed to be a law unto themselves and more concerned with the military aspects of their work than with normal police duties. At the first hint of trouble, normal police behaviour was suppresssed and they became a para-military force; the police as a symbol of normality disappeared, only to reappear ready to meet force with force. An attempt had been made earlier to discard carrying arms as a normal practice, but one armed raid on a bank had been sufficient to cause a reversal of that policy. As for the Ulster Special Constabulary, the B-Specials, Mark and Osmond emphasized that it was not a special constabulary in the sense that we would understand the term. Its whole emphasis was on firearms training, it was not integrated with the RUC, it had its own chain of command, and it was seen as a Protestant reserve army. Mark and Osmond said that in the present situation it could not be disbanded or disarmed unless something were put in its place, and they recommended that it should cease to be a special constabulary and become openly a military reserve with recruitment from all religions. In this, of course, they foreshadowed the recommendations of the Commission of Enquiry whose chairman was Lord Hunt. I was very grateful to both Mark and Osmond, whose reporting and experience were invaluable at a difficult time. Harold Wilson heard the outline of their findings from Osmond. In the afternoon I reported to a specially called Cabinet Meeting and Harold Wilson and I received their covering authority for our actions and proposals.

Later in the day we met Chichester-Clark. On our side were Harold Wilson, Michael Stewart, Denis Healey, Lord Stonham, who was a great help to me throughout this period, General Sir Geoffrey Baker, Chief of the General Staff, Sir Philip Allen, Sir Burke Trend, the Secretary of the Cabinet, and myself. Their side comprised James Chichester-Clark, John Andrews, the Deputy Prime Minister, Brian Faulkner whom Chichester-Clark had brought back into the Cabinet, and Robert Porter. The civil servants were Sir Harold Black, the experienced Secretary to the Northern Ireland Cabinet, Ken Bloomfield, the Prime Minister's adviser, who was the brains of the outfit, and B. R. Cumming, who was Chichester-Clark's Private Secretary. We met in the Cabinet Room at 10 Downing Street, a long room in which Wilson used to love to pace up and down. The two sides sat opposite each other with Chichester-Clark facing the Prime Minister.

Chichester-Clark was very good in his opening remarks and agreeably firm. He never believed in using ten words where one would do, and indeed in some of our encounters I had to prise out of him what was in his mind, not so much because he expressed himself elliptically as because he hardly expressed himself at all. But on this occasion he had clearly thought out his position. He began by expressing his gratitude for the introduction of the troops and said that although there had been a marked improvement in the situation, he had to tell us that the troops could not be withdrawn because the police were now discredited among a section of the population. He then proposed that General Freeland, the GOC, should take over control of *all* the security forces, including the RUC (but not of course their day-to-day criminal responsibilities) and the B-Specials. These forces had been the responsibility of the Northern Ireland Government ever since Stormont was created, and were the physical manifestation of their authority. At this point you could have heard the mythical pin drop: it was entirely unexpected for Chichester-Clark to come out with such a dramatic proposal for handing over control.

In response Wilson immediately took up the point but emphasized that any arrangement could only be short-term until confidence in the RUC was restored and that we hoped the troops could be withdrawn pretty soon. The lessons of Cyprus dominated all our minds at this time: how easy it was to get into such a situation and how difficult to get out. I then said that before we could agree to the arrangement Chichester-Clark had proposed, we needed to consider the B-Specials. What was his thinking on that? Chichester-Clark said he did not intend to use them for crowd control and that had never been his intention, but the sudden riots had left him short of men on August 14 in Belfast, and the Northern Ireland Government had thought it proper to use all their own resources before calling on the troops. Porter interposed that 485 B-Specials had been used in Belfast and 250 in Londonderry.

Healey said that the GOC believed there ought to be central control over the B-Specials' arms. Would General Freeland have this authority under what Chichester-Clark was proposing? Well, said Chichester-Clark, there would be a lot of difficulty about that. He was not at all sure that we would get the arms out of their hands. Indeed, in the country areas there was no doubt that the B-Specials would feel that their lives would be endangered if they lost their arms. Healey said the GOC's view was that the B-Specials had used excessive force during the rioting and that in general they were making the task of the troops more difficult. If the Army was going to take over all responsibility for security, a change in policy with regard to the B-Specials would have to be announced at the same time.

Chichester-Clark demurred at this. Changes in the role of the Specials, he said, would have to be introduced gradually or it would create too much trouble. I then proposed a two-stage operation: the Specials should be disarmed immediately but their standing down could be announced at a later stage. There was some difference in emphasis between Harold Wilson and myself about this which came out later when he went on television and appeared to say that the Specials would be disarmed and disbanded at the same time.

Before we left the subject of the police, Chichester-Clark said he was afraid that the inquiry into the RUC which we had talked about before might lead to the resignation of some senior officers and would therefore lower morale. He wanted to discuss the inquiry with the Inspector-General, although he agreed that it should be conducted by someone from Britain.

I then opened up a new salient by suggesting that we should send a civil servant of deputy secretary level to be attached to the Prime Minister's office in Stormont Castle, and another, perhaps an under-secretary, to be attached to the Ministry of Home Affairs. They would, I said, help each of us to have a perfect understanding of what the other was wanting to do. Of course what was in my mind was that these two civil servants would be able to bring very direct influence to bear on the policies of the Northern Ireland Government. This was a new thought for Chichester-Clark. He obviously did not welcome it, but said he could see there were advantages in it and he would have to discuss it with his colleagues.

I won in the end, but I lost the next point I made, which was could he not broaden the base of his government? They had had an Ulster Unionist Government for fifty years with nobody but pure party men in it. Could he not, in the circumstances, find non-Ulster Unionists to join his government to give it a different complexion? He said there was absolutely no possibility of that. Well, I replied, could he not get somebody in perhaps as a Minister of Community Relations – somebody who was not an Ulster Unionist, who would be responsible for representing in the Cabinet the views of people who belonged to the minority and were not Ulster Unionists, or might even be Protestants but not Ulster Unionists. He said he would consider the matter but he could not see much prospect of the idea of a Minister of Community Relations being accepted.

At this point – we had been talking for about an hour and three-quarters – we decided on an adjournment. We sat where we were while they withdrew to another room. Wilson ordered drinks and we went on talking among ourselves. There was some discussion between Healey and myself about the police, at the end of which we both agreed that the Army should have full control over them for the time being, provided that the Northern Ireland Government consented to an independent inquiry into the RUC; that the GOC was given full control over the B-Specials; and that there would be a rapid removal of B-Specials from duties in the cities.

Although we did not take long to reach this conclusion, the meeting did not reassemble until 8.30 p.m. because the Northern

Ireland side were having a tough session over the future of the B-Specials. When we did reassemble, Harold Wilson outlined our position to Chichester-Clark, adding the further requirement that in due course the Inspector-General should be replaced by a Chief Constable appointed from the United Kingdom. They agreed quite quickly, having obviously discussed it during their separate meeting. Chichester-Clark never argued too long once agreement had been reached. He urged that the inquiry into the RUC should not be announced until he had had a chance to discuss it with Peacocke, and the Prime Minister agreed that he should have a few days for that – the Hunt Committee was eventually announced on the 21st. It was also agreed that we would all meet again in fourteen days' time and that in the meantime I would visit Northern Ireland. We then got down to drafting the communiqué.

Harold Wilson was a master at this and also extremely keen on what he called political directives for future guidance. He was a very swift draftsman and during our discussions he had quickly written down a list of points which later formed the substance of what was to become known as the Downing Street Declaration. That morning he had handed the main points to Burke Trend and Philip Allen to dress up into a statesmanlike declaration. This he now produced, and it was agreed with only minor differences in wording to take account of various susceptibilities (see Appendix I, p. 189).

We attached very great importance to reaffirming the pledge about Northern Ireland not ceasing to be part of the UK without the consent of the people of Northern Ireland. Indeed, the Home Office would never present me with a draft speech or statement at that time without automatically including it by way of a preface. On the other hand, the statement about withdrawing troops once law and order had been restored was an expression of hope rather than of expectation. One of the most momentous passages of the Declaration was the statement that the Northern Ireland Government would take the views of HMG into fullest account at all times 'especially in relation to matters affecting the status of citizens . . . and their equal rights and protection under the law'. Such a statement may seem obvious today, but Northern Ireland was in fact acknowledging for the first time since 1922 that the UK Government's views on civil and other rights must be listened to. This sentence marked the turn of the tide in the relations between Westminster and Stormont. For forty years they had moved further and further away from the UK. Now, because they had to call on the UK for troops to sustain them, the reality of their position was uncovered, and eventually led to the suspension of Stormont itself.

One additional agreement was that the B-Specials should hold their arms at the discretion of the GOC, which was an inoffensive way of saying that the arms would be withdrawn, because the GOC had told us quite clearly that he believed they ought to hand them in. However, this led to some confusion in the light of Harold Wilson's broadcast on television that evening. He had left to do the broadcast in the hope of calming things down in Northern Ireland while our meeting was still going on. We were still drafting the communiqué in the Cabinet Room when somebody came and said, 'Harold's on the air,' and the group of us crowded into a small room where we could crane over one another's shoulders to watch. Chichester-Clark was the only one not there because he had left to make a television appearance immediately after Wilson. The Prime Minister's words were that the B-Specials would be 'phased out of their present role', which could be, and was, taken in Northern Ireland as an announcement of their disbandment. There was some muttering in the Northern Ireland group of Ministers when he said this, although our side of the table was quite clear that the B-Specials would ultimately be phased out, but that it would be enough for the moment to announce that they were being disarmed. In the Northern Ireland view of the future, it was inevitable that the arms would be withdrawn and they would agree to that, but at that stage they could not say that the B-Specials should be phased out or disbanded. However, they were in such a state of shock and disarray at this time that nothing came of the muttering, and the issue was not raised again when the Prime Minister and Chichester-Clark came back to the Cabinet Room, and we concluded the drafting of the communiqué.

6

I count myself fortunate that during this time Lord Hailsham – at that time Quintin Hogg – was in charge of Conservative Party policy on Northern Ireland. He always gave me unstinting support in the House of Commons. He used to come to my room at the Home Office and say, 'Tell me, dear boy, what you want to do? How can I help?' This was very reassuring, for at the start of the trouble the Conservative Party's attitude was an unknown factor and Quintin himself could be very volatile. We all knew of the intolerable Tory behaviour in opposition in 1912 when they were totally unscrupulous and some of their leaders urged near treason in their venom against the Liberal Government. They had seemed ready then to support the Protestants in an armed rebellion against Home Rule. So it was a great relief that in 1969 Quintin kept his Party absolutely firm in support of the Government and I pay tribute to him. I used to take him fully into my confidence – something which was in marked contrast to Reginald Maudling's attitude when our roles were reversed and he became Home Secretary and I the Opposition spokesman on Northern Ireland. He used to say he wanted to carry on my policy and he was always very affable and ready to see me. But I never had the feeling that he told me much about his plans – perhaps there was not much to tell.

I took very great care in the House not to inflame the Conservatives on the Northern Ireland issue, as I could justly have done, by referring to past history and their part in it. So I hope I made Quintin Hogg's task easier. I based my attitude on Clem Attlee's advice to me when he appointed me Parliamentary Secretary to the Ministry of Transport in 1947. The whole interview only lasted two minutes. He said in his quiet, dry way: 'Remember, you're not playing for the second eleven any more: you're playing for the first eleven. And one other thing: if you are going to do business with somebody, don't insult him the day beforehand. Goodbye!' I still think it is good advice, especially for Ministers who have to get Bills through the Commons. I have watched two types of Ministers in the Commons: those who make brilliant speeches, raise their supporters' excitement to boiling point and infuriate the opposition at the same time; and those who plod along carefully, never raise the temperature, do not ruffle the Opposition, and are reasonable in meeting their points. They usually get their Bills through twice as fast. Attlee's is a counsel of perfection, of course, and I did not always live up to it by any means. But on this issue I tried hard, for I needed Conservative support for our Northern Ireland policy, as I shared Crossman's and Jenkins's view that if we lost it the country would be divided and an intractable problem might become insoluble.

The day after the Downing Street meeting I met my officials to consider what matters we would wish to discuss when I went over to Northern Ireland. An agenda began to emerge which included the nature of the police; allocation of houses; discrimination in employment and the prospect of more jobs; whether there should be a Minister of Community Relations; what funds could be provided to alleviate the distress that had been caused, and what could be done to bring about integrated education for Catholics and Protestants.

It was at this time that Oliver Wright, who was to become the British Government's first representative at Stormont, came back into our circle. Philip Allen had told me that the Foreign Office had a man called Wright whom they would be willing to lend us. When I asked who he was I was first told that he had been a Private Secretary at No. 10 but not much was known about him, so I was pretty unenthusiastic and went on searching for my own candidate. It was only twenty-four hours later that I discovered that the Foreign Office nominee was the Oliver Wright whom I had known in the Prime Minister's office in No. 10 in 1965. He had acted as Wilson's special envoy to Rhodesia and for the past three years had been our Ambassador in Denmark. I was immediatly excited for I knew he would be first class for dealing with Chichester-Clark and we grabbed him with both hands before the Foreign Office could change its mind. He turned out to be an excellent choice: he had natural political nous. He is irreverent, with a sardonic sense of humour and a commanding presence: he is tall and has a sort of swagger when he walks, and can get along well with most people. It was decided that Oliver Wright would sit in a room next to Chichester-Clark's at Stormont Castle and that his job would be to explain British policy to Chichester-Clark and warn him where he was likely to get into difficulties with us. He would also be able to tell us what was going on. But I did not want him there just to tell me what I could learn from other quarters. I wanted him there to put some stiffening into the administration and to broaden its outlook.

Harold Wilson had launched the idea of sending a Minister to Northern Ireland. But I was not keen: I wanted to keep the problem in my own hands. Also, I thought that a resident Minister might get us more involved in Northern Ireland than was necessary. I still hoped that Chichester-Clark and his Cabinet would themselves push through a programme of reforms, and I thought that sending in Oliver Wright and two other civil servants was a good way of exercising real control without offending susceptibilities overmuch. There were rumours at the time that the whole Ulster Cabinet might resign over the B-Specials. So we might be plunged into a very tricky situation without the knowledge or resources to take over the Administration. Throughout that time my public attitude was that it was Chichester-Clark who was making the decisions even while, privately, I was chivvying them through. In the end, Harold Wilson left the decision about a Minister for Northern Ireland to me, so it never went any further.

Not surprisingly, after the Downing Street talks there was a great deal of criticism of Chichester-Clark in Northern Ireland. Paisley said the time had come for Protestants to band together again as they had done in 1912; Craig, the former Minister of Home Affairs, called for the Government's resignation; and Brian Faulkner said there was no question of the B-Specials being phased out, stood down or disbanded. I could see that tension was beginning to crystallize round this issue and that from now on the future of the B-Specials would be the focus of criticism. To offset this it was necessary that we should at once set up the Committee of Inquiry into the future of the RUC and the B-Specials. The search was on for a Chairman who would command general confidence. Harold Wilson had suggested Lord Hunt, better known as Sir John Hunt, who was the leader of the expedition which first conquered Everest. I knew and greatly respected his work, for he was also Chairman of the Home Office Parole Board. I was very glad of Harold Wilson's flash of inspiration and was grateful to John Hunt for taking on such a difficult task without hesitation, but he is of course a man of very great public spirit. Of course, technically it was the Northern Ireland Government that appointed the Hunt Committee, but the truth is that Chichester-Clark and I were working so closely together at this point that ideas might come from either of us and the other took no offence. In the matter of the police he was himself convinced that the force needed a substantial reorganization, for when the test came a third of the population were bitterly opposed to the police and they could not handle the subsequent trouble. He had lost confidence in Peacocke, so it was not difficult to convince him that John Hunt ought to head the committee of inquiry. It was announced on August 26, a week after the Downing Street meeting, and its terms of reference were to 'examine the recruitment, organiza- tion, structure and composition of the Royal Ulster Constabulary and the Ulster Special Constabulary and their respective functions and to recommend as necessary what changes are required to provide for the efficient enforcement of law and order in Northern Ireland'. Two senior policemen were appointed to assist Lord Hunt. One was Robert Mark, joint author of the preliminary report on the RUC I have already described, who later became Commissioner of the Metropolitan Police; the other was Sir James Robertson, then Chief Constable of Glasgow, whose appointment was intended to be a reassurance to the Protestants because he knew and was known in Northern Ireland. Later, when we came to discuss Peacocke's successor as Inspector-General, Chichester-Clark pressed Robertson's claims strongly.

Much time over the next few days was taken up with preparing for my visit to Northern Ireland, which was due to begin on August 27 and which I was determined would be a cocked-hat affair. I wanted the occasion to have all the majesty that Westminster and Her Majesty's Government could command. So I asked the Governor, Lord Grey, if he would kindly consent to meet me at the airport and I asked Chichester-Clark if he would do the same. Lord Grey was naturally a little reluctant. I don't think he thought it was proper for him to come, but in the end he agreed and I was grateful. So everybody was drawn up on parade as it were, and it gave the visit a dramatic start. I thought a sense of occasion and of public display was important at a time like that – and might bring success closer.

A few days before I arrived, Harold Wolseley, the Belfast Police Commissioner, told the Press that he would like me to use an armoured car if I intended to visit the trouble spots. I let it be known that I was not going anywhere in an armoured car: I was sure that it would have been a psychological error at that time to parade up and down the streets in armoured cars separated entirely from the people. For the same reason, I declined kindly offers of official hospitality from both the Governor and the Unionist Government. Instead, the Home Office took over a floor of the Conway Hotel which is set in attractive grounds just outside Belfast. Chichester-Clark came in to see me urgently one evening and was astonished at the efficiency of the set-up that the dozen Home Office staff had erected so quickly.

First among my colleagues was Lord Stonham. I am sorry to say that occasionally I used to feel a little inward impatience because I knew what he wanted to say when he was only half way through a sentence. But I tried not to show it because he was so totally loyal, hard working and selfless, and I count myself lucky to have had him with me. Unfortunately he had shortly before suffered the first of several heart attacks so he could not come round in the rough and tumble with me as he wanted to. He did something just as useful. He would spend hour after hour patiently and courteously receiving a series of deputations from the Orange Order, the Civil Rights Association, trade union groups, the Churches, and many others. He did a magnificent job in a quiet way because he was very good at making people feel that he really understood and cared about what they were saying to him. His inward sympathies were rather with the Protestants, although he became very angry about the treatment of the Civil Rights March at Burntollet.

The other politician in the team was Roland Moyle, MP for Lewisham, who was my friend and joint Parliamentary Private Secretary with Gregor Mackenzie. I noted him at an early stage in the House of Commons because he showed all the signs of inheriting the diplomacy and political shrewdness of his father, Lord Moyle, who had for many years been Clement Attlee's Parliamentary Private Secretary. He was obviously suited to keep in touch with the Northern Ireland Labour Party and trades unions and, having a good intelligence service, made regular reports on the state of feeling in the shipyards and factories.

Among the civil servants was Neil Cairncross, a draftsman par excellence who could always be relied upon to distil the maximum agreement from a discussion and produce a sheet of paper at the drop of a hat with the right form of words on it to satisfy the parties. There was Alec ('Butch') Baker, who had been a Group Captain in the RAF and who seemed to have the knack of doing without sleep and appearing in the morning after a night's work as imperturbable as ever with the same cheerful smile creasing his face. If ever I were in a tight corner and wanted someone with me whom I knew would remain calm and get on with the job, Butch Baker would be my man. Then there was Tom McCaffery, the Home Information officer and a man I relied on more than most. He was respected by the Press because while he could not always give all the information that the Press wanted, he never gave them misleading answers or sent them off on a false trail, and they appreciated this. He was quiet and self-effacing but also had some un-civil-service-like qualities, for he knew how to interpret the opinion of the man on the Clapham omnibus. After I got to know him in 1967-8 I started bringing him into discussions as an equal participant at the Home Office on almost every topic. At first there was a slight resistance from some of the other civil servants, but they too came to value genuinely his opinion and judgement. There is a variety of practice among Ministers about these things. Some Ministers leave their information officers to wait in an anteroom and then tell them what to say when a meeting is over. I don't think it is the best way if you want the information officer, and through him the Press and the public, to have a true feeling of what is happening.

I am in danger of distributing too many bouquets but truly I had an excellent team and the fierceness of the crisis brought out the best in them. Among them were Robin North, quiet and unassuming, who had specialized on Northern Ireland matters for twenty years, and John Mackay, a Home Office Inspector of Constabulary, whom we based in Northern Ireland to act as liaison between the Army and the RUC. The heroes of that period were a small group of officials who really saved the situation when it looked as if anarchy would prevail. They would not stop working – I remember on my second visit to Northern Ireland one of our shorthand-typists lost a stone in seven days – and because the pace was so intense it was exciting and somehow even enjoyable. We all felt we were doing something vital to save lives and restore peace. Certainly in simple, human terms it was the most meaningful experience of my political life. There are very few occasions in politics when you get the opportunity to handle something in your way: action usually comes after a long process of consultation, whittling down, compromise, arguing here, consulting there. In August 1969 the situation required me to exercise real authority, to do it quickly or be swamped. We had to take the initiative to restore the situation and I was moving with tremendous speed all the time. It was a most enviable position for any politician to be in: the Cabinet was on holiday, Harold Wilson was back in the Scillies, Parliament was not in session, and there was I in charge, pulling levers here, pushing levers there, saying get this, fetch so-and-so, and the whole machine absolutely buzzed. I do not think the Home Office had been so exhilarated in years. In the evenings, when we had reached a point of absolute exhaustion, I used to go out with my officials to a meal and we would discuss the events of the day in a relaxed way and sometimes even managed to wring some humour out of the situation before going back to the Home Office to cope with the urgent messages until midnight and beyond.

Although we had had long discussions at the Home Office before leaving for that first visit to Belfast, there was not at that stage any real long-term planning: we were living from hand to mouth and making policy as we needed to. Basically, my short-term aim was to try to restore a sense of self-confidence in the Ulster Unionist Cabinet, which appeared to be sunk in apathy, and to calm the fears of the Catholic community without awakening those of the Protestants. On the day I arrived, I said I did not reckon to solve the problems of three hundred years in three days: the most I could hope to do was to buy time in a situation that had become tinder-dry.

The visit started with a very elaborate press conference at Aldergrove airport, with the biggest battery of cameramen and news-papermen that Northern Ireland had ever seen. I began by saying that it was clear that deep-seated and genuine feelings of injustice and discrimination existed in Northern Ireland. No society could be stable unless those fears were examined and, if they were found to be justified, removed so as to ensure fair play for all. I was quite clear that the fears were justified and therefore I wanted to discuss with the Northern Ireland Government how they could be removed. I said I had not come to dictate: I had come to help. Only they could decide if they were willing to live together in peace, friendship and equality with one another and without discrimination. I said I wanted to be a catalyst – the agent that sets others in motion. At the back of my mind, of course, I still did not want Britain to get more embroiled in Northern Ireland than we had to. The Press and others were warning us that Ireland was a quagmire and I needed no reminder. So I tried to get people to look forward rather than back. From this time on we were engaged in a strenuous battle to win the hearts and minds of the Catholic population and to prevent them from falling into the despair that would give the terrorists their chance. Up to the time I left office I felt confident that the battle could be won, but events in the summer of 1970 and later dispelled that hope.

The press conference got tremendous coverage throughout Ireland. By contrast with the spokesmen for the Ulster Government, who were not very good at getting through to people on television and radio, I appeared to be talking with confidence, certainty and firm-ness. I tried to convey a sense of the authority of Westminster, that I knew what had to be done and would see that it was done. Some of the newspapers reported that I was greeted as though I was a saviour, but this was only by contrast with the fumbling of the Ulster Unionist Government who were limp in the extreme. Some Cabinet members had little idea of what was going on. They did not go into the Catholic areas even when all was quiet, and it was only when I walked round the streets in the Falls Road area of Belfast on the same afternoon that I fully realized the horror of what had happened in the riots. I fear our senses have since become dulled by the steady trail of atrocities, but at that time it was new to Britain and it made a tremendous impact on me. By contrast, I found a dreadful feeling of inertia and complacency in the Ulster Cabinet.

Straight after the press conference I went to Government House at Hillsborough, a few miles outside Belfast, to have lunch with Lord Grey, making an official bow, as it were, to the Governor. I then hurried back to Belfast for my first meeting, which was with representatives of the Church of Ireland, the Presbyterians and the Methodists. The Rev. Dr John Carson, of the Presbyterians, started off by saying that the Protestant churches shared a common sense of shame for what had happened. They acknowledged their mistakes; the provocations had come from both sides. A Methodist, the Rev. Eric Gallagher whom I came to know well and to like, spoke of an unofficial community relations liaison committee that had been established jointly by Catholic and Protestant priests and clergymen which had been operating for some time. Such was the state of opinion that he asked me to keep this confidential as both sides thought it sensible that it should not be known that Catholic and Protestant clergy were working together. I was astonished that they thought such a desirable matter needed to be kept secret. They said they would like to see greater Catholic participation in the life of the community. When I asked what that meant, one of them told me that there was a provision at Stormont for a Catholic priest to take part in prayers but the Catholic hierarchy had never appointed such a priest. I discovered later that Chichester-Clarke was concerned about this too and he brought the subject up in talks with me. So this was the level at which I began. Later, when I had got to know Cardinal Conway and he believed that I was going to try and help, I told him about this problem and said, 'Look, why don't you appoint a priest?' He said he would try to do so and was as good as his word. In time he did appoint a priest. But it was astonishing to find that this irritation had been festering for years.

A theme I developed with the churchmen and to which I constantly returned was that the Protestants, the majority, would have to make the first gesture if confidence was to be restored. After all, they had been in control for fifty years and were likely to remain in control, so if they really wanted to reconcile the minority it was up to them to make a gesture.

On the day that I arrived in Northern Ireland Chichester-Clark had recalled Parliament and informed them that a tribunal was to be set up under Sir Leslie Scarman, a British High Court judge, to inquire into the violence and civil disturbance which had occurred during the six months from March to August 1969, picking up, as it were, from where the Cameron commission had left off. It was important at that stage to be seen to be up and doing and so as not to lose momentum I asked Lord Gardiner, the Lord Chancellor, if Sir Leslie could fly to Belfast the next day and he very kindly did so. Naturally, he could not do much except meet the two other members of the tribunal, but it was an indication to the public that things were moving and that we were getting the situation under control. The day after that it became public that I had ordered the enquiry under Sir Harold Himsworth into the effects of CS gas, which had been used by the police in Londonderry on August 13 and 14. Again, this gave the impression that things were being taken in hand.

After the meeting with the Protestant clergy I went to walk about the riot areas. It was one of the most traumatic, emotionally draining experiences I had ever had. First, Gerry Fitt, the MP for Belfast West, took me into the Catholic area, squeezing through a gap about eighteen inches wide in a corrugated iron barricade. As we moved down the street it was often difficult to see what had happened because there was such a press of people around us. I could feel among them a terrible sense of fear and hopelessness. They wanted reassurance, even to touch me or shake me by the hand. Even so, there was one man in the crowd who shouted I was just a bloody Englishman. I retorted that on the contrary I had represented Cardiff, the capital city of Wales, for twenty-four years, which raised a laugh and he was shouted down by others in the crowd.

Another incident concerned three plainclothes RUC men. I had taken to Northern Ireland the two Metropolitan Police detectives who never left me, but unbeknown to us three RUC men had attached themselves to the rear of the party. This was ill-advised and I was told later by accompanying newspaper correspondents that when they were recognized they were hustled out of the area, which gave me an indication of how the police were regarded and of their difficulties.

I had seen scenes of devastation before in the Blitz, and early in

1946 I had visited both Berlin and Stalingrad, so I do not pretend that the Falls Road in any way resembled those. Even so, I was constantly reminded of wartime scenes. Never before in the UK had I walked past ruined houses and burned-out buses and lorries and picked my way over broken paving stones, examining bullet holes and all the other marks of violence, destruction and civil disturbance. It influenced me strongly that all the destruction was in the Catholic areas, for there was no evidence that any Protestant homes had been burned down. Eventually I was able to break away and go to another Catholic area in a constituency represented at Stormont by Paddy Devlin. Here again the crowds were so huge and so emotional that Devlin had to climb on to the bonnet of my car, where he half stood, half kneeled, and use the force of his personality, which is pretty considerable, to try and clear a way through the crowds for the car. Eventually I was able to leave the area and I walked on to Agnes Street, part of a Protestant area, and went into a small house to meet a group of Free Churchmen, Ministers and others. A group of Protestants stood outside and sang 'For he's a jolly good fellow', which was indicative of the general feeling of relief on both sides at that time – even if it did not last. I walked down the Shankill Road but the crowds were much thinner than in the Catholic areas. And whereas the Catholics had barricaded themselves into their ghetto, in the Shankill Road the traffic was flowing normally, the buses were running, and the shops were open. Women came up freely as I stood on the pavement and, shopping-bags in hand, told me how horrifying they had found the violence. I felt no antagonism towards me, although it was altogether a much less emotional welcome than in the Catholic area.

From these street scenes I went straight to my first meeting with the Ulster Cabinet. After it was over a Home Office official said it was like watching a man play tennis against an opponent who never hit the ball back. He was right. I was pushing out ideas and suggestions throughout the session, asking why did we not do this or that, and they sat and listened, apparently accepting most of what I was saying with hardly any discussion. I had arrived late and unwashed for the meeting after all the turmoil and emotion of the Falls Road and the Shankill, and the first thing that struck me was the contrast between the atmosphere of raw hatred and fear I had just left

and the somnolent air of the Cabinet. We met in a very pleasant, cool, quiet, high-ceilinged room, with the sun shining in and a view across immaculately tended lawns. And only four or five miles away was a situation which they showed no sign of understanding. I felt they should have been there in the middle of it. Some time later, after I had suggested this, Chichester-Clark did go, but even then his security guard stopped him going any further when he reached the last Union Jack in the street. So he visited only the Protestant and not the Catholic areas, and I fear the truth is that an outsider could go where a Unionist Cabinet Minister could not.

Basically, my task at the Cabinet meeting was to get to know them, reassure them, make them feel they had a role to play, that the situation was not as hopeless as they seemed to think it was, and that if only they would act quickly they would get results. I did not know Chichester-Clark very well then, although as the months went by and we understood each other we became more intimate. In the early days he was always extremely courteous and behaved like the typical upper-class Englishman would in such a situation – urbane, reserved and neither friendly nor unfriendly. Then there was John Andrews, the deputy Prime Minister, a man of goodwill, very bluff, who did his best to make me feel that I was at home, while representing very strongly that he was with the Ulster Unionists. Brian Faulkner sat at the end of the table and said very little at that meeting, although it was clear from his occasional intervention that Chichester-Clark knew even then that he had got to carry Faulkner with him in everything he did. Robert Porter was a quiet, very liberal-minded Queen's Counsel, and Phelim O'Neill, the Minister for Agriculture, who later joined the Alliance Party, was full of common sense and also of contempt for most of his colleagues. He wore a slight air of detachment from the rest. A man I could not get on with was Basil Kelly, the Attorney-General, whom I found a most difficult right-wing gentleman. I had to be very rough with him the next day over some men they had arrested under the Special Powers Act after the rioting and whom I suggested should either be charged or released. That was one of the few occasions when the iron fist came out of the velvet glove.

The first thing I discussed with the Cabinet was the Cameron Report on the earlier disturbances of 5 October 1968-11 January 1969 which was to be published shortly (see Appendix II, p. 193). I had previously raised this with Chichester-Clark as I knew that its conclusions would be that the troubles had been caused by a rising sense of continuing injustice among the Catholics over discrimination in housing and local government; that local government boundaries had been deliberately manipulated; that Catholics felt rejected; that their complaints were ignored; and that they resented the B-Specials as a partisan and para-military force. I said that this would provide ammunition for more trouble and I asked them what they proposed to do. Chichester-Clark replied in the nicest possible way that he hoped the lull we were now enjoying would lead not to more violence but to peace. He said it was very difficult to know what he and the Northern Ireland Government could do to reduce tension. They had no further reforms to suggest and they looked to time to heal the division. I was appalled, having come straight from the streets and seen the atmosphere there, and said that in my view the lull was temporary and we had only a short time to try to build something more permanent before disorder broke out again.

Porter then made a very helpful contribution. He said that if the Army would remain in control of the streets for the time being and the police were reorganized and rehabilitated in the minds of the minority, then peace could be restored. He hoped that the Hunt Commission would lead to the creation of an English-type police force and that the RUC could drop its para-military role. Naturally I was attracted by this proposal because it was in line with my own thinking. I tried to soothe any ruffled feelings by explaining that the proposed inquiry was no reflection on the RUC but that after fifty years of existence its structure, like that of most other organizations of similar age, could well bear re-examination. I said I wanted to see the police as citizens in uniform, serving the whole community and not just part of it, and that as long as a significant minority of the community felt that the police did not serve them, the police could not function successfu.ly. As regards the B-Specials, the Cabinet seemed somewhat reassured because some were beginning to hand in their arms without trouble. General Freeland had indicated that there might be a role for them for some time ahead and that arms would be issued again if and when the men were needed to guard installations.

I have wondered since whether it was some tactical consideration that prompted Chichester-Clark to say they had no proposals for any further reforms, because he and his colleagues wanted me to make the running. But I think not. The Cabinet were decent men entirely out of their depth. They were ready to go along with someone who had positive ideas. Among the flurry of suggestions I put that afternoon, the one that caused the greatest consternation was my proposal that there should be a single authority for the allocation and building of houses. They regarded the idea with near horror both on political and administrative ground, for of course it went to the heart of political patronage. But I pointed out to them that Northern Ireland's population was very little bigger than Birmingham's and that Birmingham's housing programme was centrally controlled, and so gradually brought them round to being willing to consider it. I asked them to consider this and other ideas and said we would talk about it when I met them again in two days' time. There did not seem much point in trying to carry it further that day because they needed time to accustom themselves to the proposals.

Chichester-Clark said that the Cabinet were a little concerned about the visit I proposed to pay to the Bogside the following day. I would be asked when I got there to abolish Stormont and introduce a period of direct rule. I replied that I would say in the Bogside exactly what I had said to the Cabinet: that there was no prospect of HMG agreeing to abolish Stormont at that stage and that our aim was to work through the Northern Ireland Government, getting them to bring in some very necessary reforms. I took the opportunity to inform the Cabinet that we had contingency plans prepared should law and order break down completely and Stormont be incapable of functioning. I wanted them to understand that we were ready to use those powers although we would be very reluctant to do so.

Although I hope I did not show my feelings, I found it difficult to take seriously the idea that the Northern Ireland Cabinet and Prime Minister bore any resemblance to what we in Britain understood by those offices. It was always in my mind that, by British standards, the Northern Ireland Cabinet and Parliament was little more than an enlarged county council, with rather greater powers for raising taxes and spending money and with an unhealthy political control over the police. They took seriously the notion that the doctrine of collective responsibility must apply simply because they were called a Cabinet, and used this to reject a proposal I made very early on that Catholics should be invited to join the Administration. I am glad that Mr Whitelaw rejected this doctrine.

It was early evening before I withdrew for the next event of the day, which was a dinner I gave at my hotel. Present were the leaders of the Catholic, Protestant and Methodist churches, MPs of all parties, trade unionists, and leaders of the Orange Order. It was a noteworthy occasion for leaders with such widely different views to agree to come and I had my first experience of the remarkable facility the Irish have for being violent enemies and yet being able to sit down together and enjoy a most animated dinner. Of course I was treading on eggshells. Two matters of protocol in particular concerned me, which I thought might wreck the whole proceedings. One was who should say grace; the second was should we have the loyal toast? In the end I decided we would pay our respects to God, and hoped the Sovereign would forgive a certain informality at the end of dinner. But who to choose between Cardinal Conway, the Catholic Primate; Dr Simms, the Archbishop of Armagh; and Dr Carson, Moderator of the Presbyterian Church? I settled the issue by myself saying the simple grace that we used to repeat before meals at home when I was a boy, and the distinguished clerics all solemnly intoned 'Amen'. As for the loyal toast, I did not know at the time, and no one could tell me, whether Cardinal Conway or the Republicans would regard it as an affront. When we got to know each other I soon realized that they would have been in no way put out. Anyway, I said to Cairncross, Moyle and Oliver Wright, the smokers in our party, 'For heaven's sake follow the American habit and light up as soon as you have got your soup so that it will be quite clear that the dinner is proceeding on a basis of informality.' They loyally smoked themselves dry throughout the meal.

After dinner I gave an account of why I was visiting Northern Ireland and what I hoped for. I said in particular that as the majority owed a duty to the minority, so the minority at least owed a duty to acquiesce in the constitution. This was the first public indication of my growing awareness that in winning back the Catholics we could not afford to lose the Protestants. Cardinal Conway said at once that he regarded attempts to remove the border by force as wrong and he would have no hesitation in saying so publicly. The Catholics, he added, did acquiesce in the constitution. I thought this was a very encouraging start. He said that reforms that were in hand had not come through quickly enough and did not go to the roots of the problem. As regards a reformed police force, he was sure that the Catholics would support it and join it, but he rejected my suggestion that there should be a beginning to integration of education. He thought this was only a marginal factor, and that everyone wanted their children brought up according to their own beliefs. I did not accept this in the context of Northern Ireland and at the Labour Party Conference some weeks later I emphasized its importance, to the annoyance of a few Catholics in the Labour Party. As a start, I wanted the various sixth forms to meet to discuss civic affairs, followed perhaps by extra-mural activities that would bring them together. Then I hoped that we could gradually bring together the younger age groups, recognizing this was a long-term plan.

'Billy' Blease, a man who was never blinded by faction and who represented the Trade Unions, said the police needed to be separated from the Unionist Government and that a commission ought to be appointed to control them in the way that police forces in Britain are controlled by local police authorities. This was something that I had very much in mind and I was glad to hear the idea coming from him. We tended to forget that one of the reasons why the Catholics so disliked the police was that they saw them as an arm of the Ulster Unionist Party.

Gerry Fitt, who said that he wanted a united Ireland, but not one united by force, complained that the Opposition was never properly treated as an Opposition at Stormont but was always pushed to one side, and I agreed that this was a genuine grievance.

Sam Napier, who represented the Northern Ireland Labour Party, said many Protestants regarded the State and all its institutions, including the police, as their own property. What was needed was a justified conviction that the Government was being carried out for the benefit of all the people and not just some of them. I thought that was a fair criticism too.

The company was generally agreed that the reform of the police was the first and most important measure to be taken. Roy Bradford, the Minister of Development, who represented the Cabinet at dinner, said we could not expect the Government to commit itself in advance to accepting the Hunt recommendations, although they would be considered conscientiously. I said I fully understood that and I had not asked them to accept them in advance – although privately I was quite sure that they would find it difficult to turn them down. Bradford said he thought that the influence of the Orange Order on the Unionist Government had been much over-played. He himself belonged to the Order but did not go to any of the meetings and did not attach much significance to his member-ship. On the other hand, he was candid enough to admit that if he resigned from the Order he was sure he would lose influence rather than gain it.

And so the dinner came to an end. It was all conducted in an extremely friendly and relaxed atmosphere. It was the first meeting for some time between such a broad spectrum of Protestant and Catholic leaders and at the time it contributed towards a lessening of tension. The news photographers and television cameramen were outside the hotel filming the guests as they arrived and again when I saw them off. The media were very helpful because when the public saw this mixed group coming and going it helped to create the feeling that things were being done, that people were working to-gether again, and that we were regaining a grip on the situation.

Pursuing my idea of the need to keep up the momentum of events, I asked Cardinal Conway and Dr William Philbin, the Roman Catholic Bishop of Down and Connor, to have breakfast with me the next morning. Normally I am not at my best at this time of day, but it was a beautiful, sunny morning and all the hotel staff were alert and eager to help and insisted on us having a large break-fast – enough for a week. It helped us to relax and to explore ways of overcoming the Catholic sense of fear and inferiority. At this, my first meeting with him, Bishop Philbin was not as forthcoming as the Cardinal, more strictly orthodox and unbending, but later when it came to persuading the Catholics to pull down their barri-cades, he was a very great help. I believe he had gained confidence in our intentions, as time went on.

Later that morning I met Ian Paisley for the first time, a confrontation which had been heralded by the Press as a most momentous event. In truth it was undramatic, yet it was important. He was supposed to come in for fifteen minutes but in the end stayed for forty. I had intended our conversation to be informal, like the others I had, but his wife, whom he had brought with him, said very little and sat with a shorthand notebook writing down everything we said, so I thought I should have an official note-taker too.

Paisley's view was that the leaders of the Civil Rights Movement were really interested in subverting the constitution. He knew Protestant grass-roots opinion because he had the largest Protestant church in the United Kingdom, with an attendance of over two thousand every Sunday evening. The defence of the constitution was what people were really concerned about. Bread-and-butter issues, even unemployment, did not count. I asked him what his attitude was to the programme of reforms. He said he did not like the word reform but he did not object to change provided it did not affect the fundamentals of the constitution. Did he agree with one man one vote in local government elections? He said he did, but he considered that everyone who had a vote should pull his weight in the State. I said I thought that was a pretty fair comment. Then he went on to say something that I found very odd. He said the real truth was that in many ways discrimination existed not against the Catholics but against the Protestants. He based this, so far as I could see, on the case of a lady who lived in the Protestant district of Sandy Row and whose home had been ransacked by the military. He made great play of this, but I said it sounded a little far-fetched to base such a far-reaching conclusion on such slender grounds. However, I asked him whether he would welcome the establishment of machinery to make discrimination against either Protestant or Catholic impossible in the allocation of housing and jobs? He is honest in discussion and, driven by the logic of his own argument, he had to say that he would.

Then he complained that although people like Gerry Fitt said they did not want the border altered by force, in fact their actions showed that they did. I replied that at dinner the night before Cardinal Conway in mixed company had publicly said that he acquiesced in the constitution and would not change the border by force. The note of the meeting says, 'Mr Paisley appeared impressed at this.' He went on to say that if there was this change of attitude perhaps they might sing 'God Save the Queen' in Catholic schools as a practical demonstration of their willingness to support the constitution. I said I did not think that was likely.

Then I asked him what measures he or the Protestant community could take to promote peace and reassure the minority. He became very negative, saying he was not a member of the Ulster Unionist Party and had no influence whatever. I said that sounded pretty pessimistic. He had just been telling me that he had the largest congregation in his church on Sunday evenings and yet he seemed to be accepting the complete cleavage of the communities. 'Of course you have influence,' I told him, 'and you should use it.' I said I had been deeply shocked by the passions I had seen in Belfast between what were basically the same people. 'You go into a house on the Protestant side of the line,' I said, 'and you see two rooms up and two down, an outside toilet and no bathroom.' These were basically the same people with the same problems. 'You know, Mr Paisley,' I said, 'we are all the children of God.' 'No we are not, Mr Callaghan,' he replied. 'We are all the children of Wrath.'

That flummoxed me, so I steered rapidly away from theology and decided instead to read him a curtain lecture. I ought to say that up to that moment he had done at least seventy-five per cent of the talking, and I had interrupted only to put questions. I had intended to try and get the measure of this vivid personality and I found myself liking him more as the discussion went on. So I said, 'Look, Mr Paisley, let's make a bargain. I will listen to you for as long as you want to talk provided you will then give me five minutes without interruption. And even after that, I promise that you can have the very last word after I have finished.' 'All right,' he said. 'Done.' And he smiled a great smile and launched into the attack.

When he stopped, I used my five minutes to say that I had spoken frankly to everybody I had met and I proposed to do the same with him. 'I don't feel there has been much of a meeting of minds between you and me,' I said, 'less so than between anyone else I have met so far. And I think I ought to tell you that in my view the public attitude you are taking has inflamed the situation. You stand fast on the biblical principles in which you believe, and I would be out of my depth if I attempted to argue those with you. But those principles surely enjoin on you a Christian responsibility to assuage the fears of the minority group and to help Protestants and Catholics to live together.' I talked to him along those lines and for the first time he seemed ready to come part way to meet me. He said he wanted to assure me that he did not wish to inflame any man to passion, that he was opposed to violence and bloodshed. I said I was prepared to accept that from him, but I asked him to make it clear beyond doubt at his Sunday evening church services to the people with whom he had such influence. He said he would do so and then he added that he hoped I had spoken in similar terms to Cardinal Conway. Alas, I did not reply. I wish I had, as I could have said yes. But I took the mistakenly formal view that I was not prepared to tell Paisley what I had said to anybody else in private. It enabled Paisley to complain afterwards that I had read a curtain lecture to him, but when he asked if I had read a curtain lecture to Cardinal Conway I did not reply. He finished by asking me for an assurance that the constitution would not be suspended and direct rule imposed. I replied that there was no such intention. And so the meeting ended with me making some polite conversation with Mrs Paisley about her work as a Belfast City Councillor, at which she thawed slightly, having seemed rather dour until then.

I was told that the Press outside were disappointed that there had not been a great blow-up, and that Paisley emerged looking a little subdued.

7

My meeting with Paisley overran its schedule and I was whisked off by car and helicopter to Londonderry where we had a swift lunch at HMS *Sea Eagle*, the Royal Naval base. The Commanding Officer was Captain Morton, RN, and in conversation with him I found more understanding of what was taking place than I had gleaned from the entire Ulster Cabinet. Lieut-Colonel Millman, the Commanding Officer of the battalion was present and struck me as knowing his business too and having a good grasp of the situation. He said the troops had got on well so far but he was gloomy about the reception they might get as the weeks went by.

I then paid a quick visit to the Guildhall, where I spent some time with the members of the Londonderry Development Corporation but was really impatient to get among the people. I did not know what to expect at the Bogside but an overwhelming reception awaited me. When I got through the barricade, accompanied by the local MPs, John Hume and Ivan Cooper, a woman knelt down in the street in front of me and kissed my hand. This may sound mawkish but a gesture like that is overwhelming. It made me even more determined to serve the people of Northern Ireland – all of them.

As in the Falls Road the day before, I could see little of what I wanted to see because of the tight press of people around me. The main impression I had was of being at the centre of a whirlpool of humanity bowling down the street, in which I was swept up and carried along. With me were my two detectives reinforced by two other Special Branch officers from London, one of whom, Topper Brown, had shoulders like a Rugby forward. He bore the brunt of it and, supported by John Hume and Ivan Cooper, we moved forward, a tight little arrowhead of seven people pushing through the swirling crowds. I remember in an interval of relative calm a small grey-haired man pushed through the crowd and produced out of his pocket a fading sepia-brown photograph which he asked me to look at. It turned out to be a photograph of myself, looking very much younger, with Alf Robens, Arthur Bottomley and several others. The picture had been taken in Londonderry fifteen years earlier in 1954 when we three had come as a Labour Party delegation to look into the problems of unemployment. I examined the photograph of the three young slim men and then made some jocular remark in the bantering way politicians affect. The man looked me straight in the eye without an answering smile and said, 'Yes, you're right. This picture was taken in 1954. I was unemployed then and I have not had a day's work since.' I shall never forget that reproach.

We went on, stumbling over barricades and rubble and broken glass and Hume and Cooper kept calling to the crowds to let us through, but it was near impossible. It was exhausting for all of us. I felt then that despite the cheering it was the kind of atmosphere that could have turned sour. It could have become a very ugly scene because, like all crowds, this one would be impossible to control if something went wrong. It was an occasion where your actions had to demonstrate that although you were helpless in their hands, you trusted them completely, and the fact that an RAF helicopter was flying overhead was no particular comfort to me. I had committed myself and I had to go on. There were many people who wanted to shake me by the hand and touch me; it was a rare experience in a politician's life, a great and dramatic moment which brought home the awful responsibility I carried for their hopes and fears.

Our small party was supposed to be heading for a meeting with a deputation of Bogsiders, but I was getting very tired with the constant pushing and jostling when, out of the corner of my eye across the street, I saw an old lady standing in the door of her house. I edged slowly over to her and when at last I reached her – the crowd thinking I wanted to greet her – I said, 'May I come into your house and rest?' Her name was Grandma Diver and she was eighty-four years of age. She said yes immediately, and when I got inside I asked for a glass of water. She naturally wanted to make a cup of tea so I sat on the sofa in a little front room with Grandma Diver while her daughter-in-law, Mrs Kathleen Docherty, put the kettle on. As we talked about the situation, people kept crowding in and peering through the window while the stewards stood guard at the door. I said to John Hume that it was quite clear we could not go any further and that if the Bogside deputation wanted to see me they would have to come to Grandma Diver's. So scouts were sent out through the crowd and eventually the deputation arrived and somehow we all sat down on chairs or on the floor in the tiny front room.

I was very firm when they told me they wanted Stormont abolished. I repeated what I had told the Cabinet, that it could not be abolished. I told them without reservation, as I had told everyone else, what I was ready to do, and so we had a very frank conversation. I did not give an inch when I did not think it justified and I found that they did not resent the plain speaking. At that time we were still in the situation of telling people how far we were prepared to go, and provided you seemed to be fair-minded and trying to help, in the end they would say, 'All right, that's it.'

After a while the question arose of how they were going to get me away. There was no back door – and anyway I would not have wanted to be sneaked out – but the crowd was still pressing right up against the front window and the front door, and tightly jammed across the whole street. So I asked whether it would help if I made a short speech from the upstairs bedroom window. They thought it would. My Home Office advisers had kept discreetly in the background and could not be reached on the edge of the crowd, so I turned to Sergeant Cawthorne, one of my detectives, and said, 'Gordon, what do I say to them?' He said, 'Well, sir . . .' and stopped. That left me on my own. So I had to think fast while everyone in the room talked at the top of their voices, and waited for somebody to produce a loud-hailer. Hume and Cooper and I went upstairs, pushed aside the washstand and jug and threw up the sash window. Then they leaned out and said that if the crowd would keep quiet I would be coming to address them and that is what I did.

I told the sea of upturned faces that with their leaders in this terrace house in the Bogside, we had had as constructive a discussion as I had had with anyone else in the country. Responding then to the events of the afternoon I said: 'You have engaged my sympathies and my energies. I will try and ensure that there is justice and equality, absence of fear and discrimination. I am a realist in politics,' I went

on, 'and I know what can be done and I am not going to promise
you the earth. I will promise to do my best.' And at that moment
of speaking I made up my mind to come back again. And told them
so. There was a tremendous burst of cheering. I went on to say
that I was not on anyone's side – Protestant or Catholic. But I was
on the side of all those, whoever they were and whatever community
they might belong to, who were deprived of freedom and justice.
Then I appealed to them: 'Now you must let me go. I have other
work to do. Will you please open up a path and let me through.' The
stewards went to work quickly because I was anxious to go to the
Protestant areas, and managed to force a very narrow lane through
which we could go, two by two, slapped on the back at every step.

I set off at a spanking pace up the hill towards the gates of the
old city trying to hurry while giving the impression that I was doing
nothing of the sort. Everything happens very quickly in Northern
Ireland, and because Derry is so small, I scarcely had time to dis-
engage from the Bogside and refocus my mind before I was walking
among the Protestants in their part of the city. Fifty yards on the
other side of the city walls stood a Protestant barricade. A group
of men and women were standing around it waving Union Jacks
and as soon as they saw me they started singing 'God Save the
Queen'. I immediately stopped and stood stiffly to attention, hands
at my side. They seemed rather disconcerted by this because the
Protestants tend to sing the national anthem as a rather jolly sort
of party piece or sometimes as a menacing war cry. Seeing me standing alone at attention in no-man's-land in the middle of the street
induced, I think, a feeling that perhaps they should be a little restrained. At any rate, when they had finished singing I did not walk
to the barrier but turned aside and went over to two soldiers who
were standing at the corner and spoke to them, deliberately giving
myself a chance to adjust to a new situation. You do these things
instinctively: you cannot rationalize them or prepare for them. Only
after that did I walk up to the crowd, where I was greeted by
Commander Albert Anderson, the local Stormont MP, whom I
thought to be a nervous, unwelcoming man. I understood why when
we walked down the street and he glanced fearfully from side to
side and said, 'There is a revolver stuffed in nearly every house, you
know.'

H.D.   G

He led us to the rather drab headquarters of the local branch of the Unionist Party, where we met Major Glover, the chairman, together with a group of very strident Ulster Unionists. The difference in atmosphere was most marked. Major Glover said that the two communities in Londonderry did not want to come together, and that he did not want them to do so. I told him that whether or not the fears of both sides were justified, they were undoubtedly real. But, I said, the Protestants had a large and permanent majority and they disposed of the power. It was for them to make the first gestures if there was to be any chance of the people of Northern Ireland living together peacefully. They could not grasp this idea at all. It was even less of a meeting of minds than the meeting with Paisley earlier that day, a thoroughly depressing occasion in thoroughly depressing surroundings. It was the first time I came slap up against the virulence of rank-and-file Protestant feeling and it was a salutary lesson.

That evening, tired and a little depressed, I flew back to Belfast to attend a buffet supper I had arranged to meet industrialists, trade unionists, newspaper editors, and other leaders of opinion. They were mostly what I would call moderates, which is to say that they were well to the left of the Cabinet. It was disconcerting to me to find how contemptuous the industrialists were of Northern Ireland politicians generally and of the Government in particular. I asked them to suppose that they would be meeting the Cabinet the next day, as I would be, and tell me what ideas or demands they would put to them. First of all, they said, with a surprising unanimity, the Government should dissociate itself from the Orange Order; the Protestants should stop acting as if they owned the place; recruitment to the RUC should be in the hands of an impartial civilian committee; the British military police, assisted perhaps by British police officers, should look after the Bogside; there should be an Act prohibiting discrimination on religious grounds; and the minority should be represented in Parliament by a Minister who commanded their general support. Most of all, they were convinced that none of these things could be handled by the present Government and that if they were going to be done, then the British Government would have to turn on the pressure.

The discussion broke up some time after 11 p.m. and my officials and I held a tactical conference at midnight. Cairncross, the Under-Secretary at the Home Office, had been having talks which continued throughout the day with Harold Black, and reported that while the Northern Ireland Cabinet were likely to agree to consider my proposed programme of reforms, they were showing an unwillingness to commit themselves to a specific examination of the various items, on the grounds that they might prove to be impractical and would savour of dictation from Westminster. I said that was not good enough. I was in no particular mood at that stage to be put off by a group of people who seemed to have no conception of how close they were to disaster. I instructed Cairncross to get hold of Black, even if it meant getting him out of bed, and tell him that I would not be satisfied unless the Cabinet would agree to commit themselves to a specific programme. I also asked Cairncross to draft a communiqué during the night on the assumption that at the conclusion of the talks there would be basic disagreement between Northern Ireland Ministers and myself. In the draft communiqué he should set down, and he should tell Black that he was doing so, the reforms that I had put to the Cabinet for examination and which they were unwilling to accept. In the absence of agreement I would make it public. And Cairncross, who was the perfect civil servant, went off to do just that.

I then undressed. I have the habit when I am shaving or undressing of stopping and jotting down notes when I think of something. So there I was in a picture window suite, walking round in my pants and nothing else, thinking and writing notes for use during the following day, and looking out over the hotel grounds. The curtains had not been drawn and suddenly there was a knock on the door and a voice said, 'Sir, the RUC man in the grounds says it would be for your greater comfort if you were to pull the curtains.' I did so at once, but was never quite sure whether he was concerned more with decorum or my security. So ended a crowded eighteen-hour day.

Early next morning Cairncross produced the communiqué he had drafted during the night. We ran through it together at breakfast and he went off to tell Harold Black that if they were willing to agree to the proposals then the Cabinet could say publicly that this is what they had put to me; if, however, they disagreed, the communiqué would say I had put the proposals to them and they had rejected them. I had a strong hand, for it would be the end of them if they did not fall into line, because the world's Press and public opinion in Britain would be against them, and they would be absolutely out on their own.

I had set Friday morning aside to meet the RUC and the B-Specials, and accompanied by Anthony Peacocke, the Inspector-General, who volunteered hardly a word during the morning, I first visited the Belfast police headquarters. There, Wolseley, the Commissioner of Police for Belfast, a very decent man but clearly tired and extremely worried, confirmed to me that the RUC had been unacceptable in parts of Belfast and Londonderry for the previous two years. On a large-scale map in his office he showed me which areas the RUC did not venture into freely. It is necessary to emphasize this because among the myths that have grown up is the reiterated untruth that the recommendations of the Hunt Report in October 1969 which led to the disarming of the RUC were the cause of their inability to control the no-go areas. This is not so. These areas had not enjoyed normal police protection for two years before the troubles came to a head in the summer of 1969. No policeman had gone on foot into these areas for at least two years. If they had to go they went in a patrol car. The Stormont Government knew all this but had taken no steps to correct it. They allowed the situation to deteriorate over a long period without seeking advice. or assistance from the Home Office. No one in the Home Office knew anything about it. Nor did Stormont take steps to strengthen the police. So for two years or more before 1969, parts of Belfast and Londonderry had remained almost outside the law and under their own so-called jurisdiction.

To me, that day was a powerful indictment of the evil of the political control of the RUC and of the urgent need for reform. I was appalled at the slackness of the Northern Ireland Government. Wolseley could clearly see the weakness. He told me that he wanted the RUC to be acceptable to the whole community but, given the present set-up, he had no ideas on how to achieve this. He said that the RUC as a State force – those were his words – was an obvious target for those who wished to attack the Government.

After this I visited members of the RUC's Central Representative Body and again we talked about the no-go areas. I was told that the Bogside was full of what they called queer and awkward people. They did not know, as I did, what the Cameron Report would have to say about police behaviour in the Bogside which had undoubtedly provoked queer and awkward reactions. But I was working on the basis that we would not get through our troubles if police morale remained low so I did my best to try to restore their self-confidence. I tried to show that I understood and sympathized with their difficulties, and I encouraged them to put their views on pay, conditions, recruitment and other matters that concern the man on the beat, to the Hunt Commission. I asked for and received a promise that they would do so.

After that came a meeting with the commandants of the B-Specials. These senior officers naturally would have great influence with their men in the event of trouble about the future of the force, and I therefore determined that this was to be a very formal and disciplined occasion. I requested them therefore to come in uniform. They filed into the room dressed in a motley variety. Some wore Ulster Special Constabulary uniforms – dark green with high necks – while others, former Army, Navy or Air Force officers, wore Service uniforms. Once I thought I caught a smell of mothballs. I invited them to be seated and asked what they had to tell me.

They said it was their belief that for fifty years the people of Ulster had lived under the shield of the Ulster Special Constabulary and would not have survived without it. I said, mildly, that there seemed to be a number of people who were outside that shield and did not want its support. Were they really speaking for all the people of Ulster? Well, they said, they were speaking for the majority, and if the shield of the B-Specials was removed, then many of their members would look to the Ulster Volunteer Force for protection. They said that the USC had been the victim of a propaganda campaign conducted by the Press and television, and Harold Wilson's broadcast on the night of the Downing Street meeting had given rise to fears among their men that the central storage of arms was the first step towards their disarming and disbandment. I could only agree with their conclusion, but I did not feel it prudent at that stage to labour the point.

I told them quite truthfully that I knew the majority of men they commanded were, by and large, a sober and responsible section of the community. I said that I thought their original role of protecting the frontier had been distorted by their involvement in riot control of crowds, which was a highly specialized task for which they were not intended and had not been trained. The Hunt Commission was about to review the structure of the whole force. I thought they would point the way to the future and we ought to leave them to recommend what they thought to be necessary. Once they had reported and the Stormont Government had reached its conclusions on the matter, it would be their duty as commandants of the force to use their influence to the full to ensure a disciplined acceptance of the decisions of the civil power, whatever they might be and however distasteful they might think them. They had, all of them, sworn an oath of allegiance to the Queen. The Queen's Government would take the decisions and it was their responsibility to ensure that they were carried out. While they were waiting for those decisions they should maintain a calm and disciplined acceptance of orders. The note of the meeting taken by officials says at this point: 'The commandants all appeared to have military backgrounds and were obviously affected by an appeal to discipline. Several stiffened to attention in their seats as the Home Secretary reached his peroration.' I did really lay it on the line. I was fortunate to be dealing with former officers with Service backgrounds who had been schooled in the belief that subordination to the civilian power is the dominant characteristic of the armed forces. I sometimes think we do not realize how lucky we are in Britain in this respect. Anyway, what I said had a temporary impact.

Even then I was not finished as I had two more meetings before lunch. The first was with representatives of the Nationalist Party, under their experienced and veteran leader Eddie McAteer. It was their view that the recent riots were not due, as the Prime Minister seemed to think, to Republican elements, but to the failure of the Northern Ireland Government to remedy the grievances that the people felt. The Nationalist Party said they had given the Unionists forty years to put matters right. They had not done so, and the Party now looked to the British Government to step in. They made no reference to the border. I went over familiar ground with them, saying that I came to Ulster as an outsider who wished to see peace and justice. I did not feel that I could ask people to surrender entrenched positions and I certainly could not ask the Stormont Government to surrender its independence. That would merely transform a situation in which one-third of the population was dissatisfied into a situation in which two-thirds of the population were dissatisfied. I continued to repeat that there had got to be concessions on both sides. I appealed to them to give us a breathing space: to wait, for example, the six weeks it would take Lord Hunt to complete his inquiry.

I then moved on to a meeting at Stormont with Ulster Unionist MPs. Once more I told them that I did not wish to interfere in Ulster affairs but that the British Government had inevitably become involved through the presence of British troops. The border and the future of Stormont was not an issue, but that being so, I had to draw their attention to the special obligations which devolved upon the Unionist Party with its permanent majority and unchallengeable power. Gestures had to come from those who held such an unassailable position and it was necessary to show the world that there was no discrimination in Northern Ireland. I said I appreciated that they had difficulties in persuading some of their supporters to accept the reforms but I wanted them to appreciate that we, too, were also subject to political pressure, the pressure of world opinion. It would be easier for us to defend the position of the Northern Ireland Government if it could be shown that the Government was reasonable and just. They asked that Stormont should be allowed the credit for initiating the reforms as it would be much more difficult to carry Unionist opinion if it looked as if the reforms had been forced on them by Westminster. I was in full agreement with that. The meeting went on far longer than intended and when we finally broke up, there was a not unfriendly atmosphere. Indeed despite the first shock and dismay during that period, my reception on that visit to Northern Ireland was generally friendly. Later, of course, it changed.

I then sat down to lunch with the Cabinet. We talked about our hobbies and interests and the state of the harvest and who was going sailing that weekend – all far removed from the real problems. The only item of political interest during lunch was that Faulkner, who was sitting on my right, leaned over and whispered that since my last meeting with them the Cabinet had agreed to release those detainees held under the Special Powers Act who were not going to be charged. This was good news because it was something I had pressed for and it suggested that I might have an easier passage with the Cabinet than I had feared.

The Cabinet meeting began immediately after lunch. On our side were Lord Stonham, Roland Moyle, Oliver Wright, Neil Cairncross, Tom McCaffery and myself. Thanks to Victor Stonham's negotiations with the Treasury, I was able to begin by announcing that the British Government had decided to make a contribution of £250,000 to a distress fund which had been set up by the *Belfast Telegraph* for the victims of the rioting. Chichester-Clark then told me about the release of the detainees, and after this mutually agreeable exchange, we got down to business.

I said I would like the Northern Ireland Government to make certain propositions to me, and these were that we should set up a series of joint working parties to look into specific subjects: the building and allocation of houses, discrimination in jobs, and economic development and unemployment. We would then, I said, be able to announce a substantive programme of work: Hunt was known to be examining the RUC and the B-Specials; Scarman would investigate the causes of the riots; and people would see that we were moving on from there to deal with social and economic ills. If they cared to put those propositions to me I could tell them straight away that the answer would be yes. Furthermore, recognizing that they would have manning difficulties with this burden of work, I was ready to offer them a team of British civil servants, who would serve on the working parties and help to run them. We could then announce in our communiqué that the Government of Northern Ireland had sought my co-operation in setting them up and I would go on record as saying that I thought these initiatives were extremely welcome and forward looking and deserved a positive response from all sections of the community, Catholic as well as Protestant. I would also emphasize yet again that the border was not an issue and that direct rule was not intended. Of course, I still had in my pocket at this stage the communiqué that Cairncross had drawn up the previous night which set out exactly the same programme but with an additional paragraph saying that I had put these proposals to the Northern Ireland Government who had rejected them. I was ready to bring that piece of paper out at the appropriate moment if things went wrong.

Chichester-Clark and the Cabinet listened to me intently, without interruption. At the end they asked no questions and the Prime Minister said he thought they should consider my statement on their own, and asked us to withdraw to his own room. We did, but I was so tensed and restless that I could not sit indoors and, with the sun shining brilliantly, we paced up and down the lawns at Stormont discussing what we would do if the Cabinet failed to agree. I listened to the others, but had already made up my mind in the event of failure to call in the Governor and General Freeland immediately, as between the three of us we should have had sufficient command and authority to have made some kind of start in handling the problems that would at once have arisen. I repeat that I did not want it that way, and for that reason I had been relieved at lunch to hear that they were going to release those detainees who were not to be charged. It seemed a good augury. I kept to myself my plan for involving the Governor and the GOC, so none of my party was quite decided on the next step; but everyone realized that it would be a dramatic watershed. And then after a very long hour of waiting we were told the Cabinet were ready for us.

Chichester-Clark began in his usual matter-of-fact way. They had considered these matters and were ready to make the following proposals: first, Chichester-Clark would on his own responsibility appoint a Minister of Community Relations; second, a series of working parties should be set up to consider (a) how to prevent incitement to religious hatred, (b) the functions of a new Community Relations Board whose members would be half Catholic and half Protestant, (c) discrimination in public employment, (d) the allocation and building of houses, and (e) economic questions.

Common sense had won. I disguised my elation as I made a few formal but friendly remarks welcoming their decision. Both of us agreed that we would have to put a very strict time-limit on the working parties, and there and then we decided to give them until October 9 to produce their reports, on which date I would return for a second visit. I think they saw the agreement as a way of preserving their own independence. Besides, what else could they do? They certainly had few if any ideas of their own. World opinion

was against them. British troops were patrolling the streets. The
police force had collapsed. They were dazed and at the end of their
tether. And public opinion in Britain at that time certainly did not
want us to run Northern Ireland; not directly anyway. To make the
Stormont Government carry through the necessary reforms was, I
thought, the right way to do it. And, of course, by this stroke we
had forestalled the outburst that would otherwise have come when
the Cameron Commission published its conclusions in fourteen days'
time condemning inadequate and unfair allocation of houses in
Catholic areas and discrimination in local government jobs, among
other things.

It was not until much later that the Ulster Cabinet began to reassert
their independence. It happened as the first instalment of the troubles
died down and they began to recover their self-confidence, in the
spring of 1970. By then I had other preoccupations. It was not that
they tried to whittle the agreed policies away, but as conditions
became more quiet they began to take back day-to-day control. I was
conscious of a growing apprehension that there would come a
moment when they would want to take some steps which would lead
to a major difference of opinion between us. However, that still lay
in the future on that hot August afternoon as we sat down to draft
the communiqué.

Usually on these occasions you have a discreet adjournment while
the officials go away and put together a coherent and sober
statement. But we were pressed for time. It was already 6 p.m. and
it had been announced that I would go on television at seven, so we
had to get the communiqué agreed and handed to the Press, who
can be hard taskmasters, before then. So with the rest of the Cabinet
and our party standing around the room in little knots chatting
together, I sat down with Chichester-Clark opposite me and Cairncross on one side of me and Harold Black on the other. One of us
would write a sentence or two and then I would say to Chichester-
Clark, 'Now do you think this is all right, or do you think some
other form of words is necessary . . .?' and as we completed each
page a typist would come in and take it away. Sometimes one or
two of the others would lean over our shoulders to see how we were
getting on and to make suggestions. People had different ideas, and so
we had little bits of paper all around us which we stitched togethe r

The full text of the communiqué is given in Appendix III (p. 199).

As the last sheet was being typed I said to Chichester-Clark, 'We must tell the GOC and the Cardinal.' He fully understood about the GOC and we telephoned and asked him to come round. But the idea of telling the Cardinal caused some consternation. I doubt if the Prime Minister ever telephoned the Cardinal: there was generally so little communication. I was holding on to an extension as they put the call through and I could hear the flutter at the Cardinal's end too. I told the Cardinal the principal points in the communiqué and that, apart from the GOC, he was the first man to know because it was his community which was in trouble. I said I had a request to make of him. I wanted him to give his blessing to the communiqué as soon as it was announced on television. The Cardinal said that from what I had told him it sounded a very good agreement and certainly went further than he had expected. He was willing to say something that would be helpful. I thanked him very much and said I was now going to get on to the Press and the radio and television and ask them to go down to Armagh and see him forthwith. So within an hour of the communiqué coming out the Cardinal had given the Catholic community a lead. Whether they agreed with him was another matter but at least they knew his opinion and I was very grateful.

Before the press conference Chichester-Clark and I sat alone for a while in his study at Stormont Castle, a pleasant room with deep comfortable sofas, rather like a country house library, relaxing with a quiet drink. He pulled on his cigar and said by way of conversation that he was very sorry they had not offered me any hospitality, but then we had all been extremely busy. And I said, 'Yes, and what is more, James, I did not know when I came whether I would have to arrest you . . .' He did not say anything but puffed reflectively on his cigar and we turned to something else. Perhaps it was just as well that he was too much of a gentleman to ask under what powers I would have done it.

There was an air of expectancy at the press conference. I was told beforehand that the television intended to interrupt whatever programmes were on at the time in order to broadcast the proceedings live throughout Northern Ireland as they happened. I went into a long, low-ceilinged room filled with smoke and cavernous-like except where the gloom was shot through with shafts of light from the television lamps. It was overflowing with reporters from Britain, the north and south of Ireland, Europe and America, all squatting on the floor or on chairs. They treated me with an absurd respect. I was told the streets were as empty as if the Cup Final was being played.

Being aware that I had all Northern Ireland for an audience, I started off by making a long, very firm and forthright statement about what we had done and what still needed to be done and ended by repeating that I would be returning. I hoped to convey that we had a sense of direction, of control and of purpose. Then the reporters asked questions, a number of which were hostile, of course. But the man holding the press conference is at a very great advantage over his questioners as long as he knows what he is talking about, for he has the last word. And in addition, the Press had only just seen the communiqué and had had little time to master it. While I was so engaged, Oliver Wright telephoned Harold Wilson to tell him about the agreement we had concluded, and also the Foreign Office, so that they could start sending out telegrams to our Ambassadors throughout the world. I had made a point of telling the Northern Ireland Cabinet this, for in those days they had little understanding of the impact that their affairs were making on foreign countries.

When all was over I was driven to the airport and there occurred one of the most scarifying incidents of the whole trip. Our group of cars was weaving through a narrow back street somewhere in Belfast with cars parked on both sides and only enough room for a single line to go down the middle. Suddenly a woman emerged from between two cars, swayed drunkenly and fell in the street right in front of us. Fortunately our driver's reactions were swift and he pulled up in about two cars' lengths with the bumper literally an inch away from her. Gordon Cawthorne, my detective, leaped out, as did four RUC men in the car behind, picked up the woman and carried her to the pavement. We decided that my car should drive on immediately because a crowd might have assembled in a matter of seconds and it would have been rumoured that we had knocked her down. I had no idea whether she was a Catholic or a Protestant but in that sort of explosive atmosphere it would hardly have mattered. I had a report later that, as we thought, she was drunk but unharmed.

Everybody kept very quiet about it at that time and I was relieved that the Press failed to pick it up.

Looking back on the visit, I can say that in the matter of calming people down we achieved more than we had hoped for and certainly more than I had planned when the visit was first mooted at Downing Street on August 19. At that time we had little more in mind than a tour of inspection to breathe the air and generally get the feel of the situation. But as the situation deteriorated after the 19th it became clear that I had to do more than that, and events moved so quickly that for a few days it was a case of improvising and acting by instinct as the problems arose. Apart from setting up major inquiries by Scarman and Hunt, the principal achievement, without doubt, was to have secured by agreement a very great extension of Westminster influence without facing the crisis that would have arisen if the Ulster Unionist Government had resigned. To do so meant reversing a tide that had flowed strongly in the other direction for the past forty years. Certainly that was the moment at which our authority was strongest.

Harold Wilson personally gave me every encouragement throughout this period. Despite our earlier differences on the Industrial Relations Bill, he was kindness itself. He later told me that he regarded it as a turning-point in the standing of the Labour Government, for we appeared to be handling an unprecedented situation with firmness and authority.

I am very conscious as I write these words that, measured against the horrors that have taken place since, our problems and our triumphs seem relatively minor. But men's reactions to a new situation must reflect to some extent their previous experience and we had little enough experience in modern times of how to handle a part of the United Kingdom in which society seemed to be disintegrating. Perhaps fortunately, we were not case-hardened then; we did not realize how much disorder, destruction and death a society can take without its fabric actually tearing apart. We had no conception that our society could endure the sufferings of the people of Northern Ireland during the past years and still retain some sense of coherence. Since then it has become hard to struggle against the numbing effect of seeing men, women and children with shattered bodies almost nightly on our television screens. It is difficult now to recall the overwhelming sense of shock in Britain when the first shot was fired and even worse when the first man was killed . . . It goes to show how easily mankind can become debased and how quickly we can adjust ourselves to the most evil circumstances.

I was brought up to believe that democracy's foundations and civilization's roots were embedded like rocks in our society. But I do not believe that any more. Our national temperament is so sluggish – we are so tolerant about everything (except for spasmodic twitches) – that we could find the chains of dictatorship riveted on us before we bestirred ourselves. Of course our temperament, being stubborn as well as sluggish, would cause us to fight back tenaciously and, I have no doubt, to break the chains when we eventually roused. But I am more than ever aware that the prizes of democracy and of civilized conduct are secured only through eternal vigilance, and it is easier to lose them than to regain them.

8

September 1969 was the month of the barricades. I had made a very strong plea at my press conference before leaving Belfast that these should come down as a sign of a return to normality. The Catholics had erected them, after the rioting in mid-August, round their traditional no-go areas as a protection against Protestant incursion. The Protestants had erected theirs later largely as a protest, and in the belief that large numbers of IRA men were taking refuge behind the Catholic barricades. In fact the IRA at that time was almost dormant and had little support. One of the slogans I saw sprayed on walls in the Catholic areas was: 'IRA – I Ran Away.' None the less, some Ulster Unionists were anxious to ascribe all the rioting and disturbances to the IRA, as a certain means of distracting attention from the need for civil reforms. Of course many individual Republicans were active in the civil rights movement and the street protests and used them for their own ends, but it was not until later, and probably in the last two months in which we were in office, that they began to control events and to dictate the pace.

The strategy that evolved during September while the battle to remove the barricades swayed to and fro – some down one day and others up the next – was that we let it be known that we would not remove barricades that were designed for protection until we had persuaded the people behind them that the troops were present in sufficient numbers to look after them, and that they had nothing to fear. On the other hand, we said, barricades erected simply as a form of protest would have to come down. At the same time I firmly resolved that neither type of barricade was to be the subject of political bargaining. The third point in our strategy was that the Army should build our own barricade along the principal frontline between the two communities so that all the other barricades could come down automatically. This became the so-called peace line, which still stands.

We had an early example of the barricades being used as a political bargaining counter when, towards the end of August, Jim Sullivan, chairman of the citizens' defence committee in the Falls Road area and an IRA man, met General Freeland at a chapel in the Falls Road and made five demands, in return for which, he said, the Catholics would dismantle their barricades. These were: the disarming of the RUC and the disbandment of the B-Specials; the release of men who had been charged after being held under the Special Powers Act; the abolition of the Special Powers Act; an amnesty for everyone involved in the disturbances, Protestant as well as Catholic; and the immediate recall of all arms in the province, including those held under permit. General Freeland alerted me to what had passed but quite rightly made no response to those demands. The result was some increase in tension between the soldiers and the Catholic community.

The pirate radios were still giving us a lot of trouble at this time. The Protestants had a lady called Orange Lily who preached a daily hymn of hate against the Catholics. There was also someone called Roaring Meg, after the cannon on the walls of Londonderry. These two specialized in broadcasting threatening and very personal messages. They would say things like: 'Hullo, Jimmy X, I wouldn't employ those six Papists you've got in your shop any longer if I were you, unless you want a present of a petrol bomb.' They also used to warn the soldiers of the dangers of accepting 'poisoned' tea and sandwiches from Catholic housewives.

The Catholics had two stations, which did not seem to operate with quite the same efficiency as the Protestants'. One was called Radio Free Belfast; it went out from a terrace house in the Falls Road area and broke down finally through over-heating, despite desperate efforts to keep it cool by playing a woman's hair-dryer on the apparatus. The other was called Radio Peace. It was staffed mainly by students and teachers and broadcast pleas for calm between midnight and 5 a.m. Both stations tried to keep up the morale of the people behind the barricades.

The Protestant stations were far more pernicious. On September 7, for example, while a fairly minor confrontation was going on in Percy Street, Orange Lily called on every able-bodied man to go to the area, which lies between the Falls Road and the Shankill.

Protestants poured out in response to the appeal and the result was a full-blown riot during which our troops had to use CS gas.

For several days I had been asking the Post Office to take action to stop the pirates but with no result. I had naturally become increasingly impatient with this, so the next day the Army were authorized to jam the stations whenever they thought inflammatory statements were being made. We were all fearful that the legality of this would be challenged, but it was not, either in Britain or in a Northern Ireland Court, and eventually the stations closed down following constant jamming.

The building of the peace line was announced by Chichester-Clark on September 8 and the Royal Engineers began work immediately. They erected a 6 ft high curtain of corrugated iron and barbed wire which ran intermittently for about a mile and a half across streets and waste ground between the Falls Road and the Shankill. Chichester-Clark then said rather peremptorily that all other barricades would have to come down at once and a deputation of Catholics promptly flew to London to demand my support for their retention. The party included three MPs – Paddy Kennedy, Paddy Devlin and Gerry Fitt – and also Father Padraig Murphy, the parish priest of St Peter's in the Falls Road, a wonderful leader of his flock who constantly strove for peace, and Tom Conaty, a businessman. They were accompanied by Jim Sullivan, whom I knew to be a member of the IRA and whom I therefore refused to see; he waited in an ante-room.

After a rather difficult five-hour meeting we agreed on a formula; that the local Army commander would first discuss the security situation with the people behind the barricades; that he would assess the requirements for military protection and how they could best be met; and that the barricades would be removed either by the local people alone or with the help of the Army. But although we seemed to have reached agreement and when they returned to Belfast many barricades did come down, others went up almost as quickly.

After this agreement I gradually shifted my weight from reassuring the Catholics to showing understanding of the Protestants. I thought that the Catholics now had adequate protection and that their fears were less necessary than they had been. They now seemed to be exploiting those fears and I felt that the Protestants had a case for saying that since the troops were available in sufficient numbers, there was no reason why the barricades should stay. Chichester-Clark was coming under increasing attack from his own party, so on September 15, after I had talked with Harold Wilson, General Freeland was asked to come over for a meeting at 10 Downing Street to discuss the whole subject.

Afterwards I telephoned Chichester-Clark, who said that he wanted to announce again that all the barricades would come down in the next twenty-four hours and proposed to issue an ultimatum to that effect. I asked what would happen if he issued the ultimatum and there was no response. Chichester-Clark, from time to time, would get himself into a very exposed position and then have to walk backwards. His response to my question was that action would have to be taken. So I naturally inquired what action he had in mind. To this he replied that the Army should do it by force. Such a step would have undermined our whole strategy, up to that date, of getting the Catholic community to take down the barricades of their own volition, and I was certainly not too willing to see this approach completely reversed because Chichester-Clark was under pressure to change his mind. So I offered instead to make a television broadcast that night and repudiate all the political demands that were being made as a prior condition of taking down the barricades. Chichester-Clark accepted this. I therefore made a very firm statement saying that the barricades had to come down and we could not tolerate their use as political bargaining counters and reiterated that the Army would ensure protection for everybody. Fortunately those manning the barricades capitulated the very next day.

General Freeland showed very great wisdom throughout this time and it was his restrained tactics which in the end proved successful. I should add that he got very little help or understanding from the Belfast City Council, who were supposed to help him determine the route of the peace line. His comments on the quality and level of ability of the councillors and administrators were absolutely sulphurous. And I suspect that he was right. By the end of September our tactics were justified. Nearly all the barricades in both Belfast and Londonderry had voluntarily been taken down and no more than a handful remained. Unfortunately, whenever there was any fresh outbreak of rioting at a later date, they tended to reappear.

The Cameron Report on the disturbances of the previous winter was published on September 12. It found that the Catholics had suffered injustices, that sections of the police had not behaved as they should have done, and that the Government had left unremedied, grievances which should have been put right. It distributed blame among pretty well everyone involved, and one of its chief effects, paradoxically, was to strengthen Chichester-Clark's position in his own Party. It was obviously an impartial report and his Party critics for the moment were silenced by it. On the day of its publication the Northern Ireland Government issued what they called a 'commentary' on the Report. This noted that Cameron had acknowledged the 'rapid economic and social progress' made in Northern Ireland up to the previous autumn and went on to detail the various reforms put in hand since then. Although there was naturally much publicity, the Report did not arouse nearly as much anger as it might have done, for we had partially defused it by the initiatives taken during my visit the previous month.

Towards the end of September Jack Lynch made a notably conciliatory speech at Tralee in which he emphasized that force could never be a solution to partition and that he sought unity 'through agreement in Ireland between Irishmen'. Chichester-Clark, as had become customary over the past fifty years, immediately issued a lengthy reply. Although what he said was restrained and civil, the Foreign Office read it with considerable dismay. A dialogue was all very well so long as there was no trouble in the streets: North and South could conduct their verbal battles in whatever way they thought appropriate. But after the troubles in August, the Foreign Office found themselves called upon to defend the Northern Ireland Government's policies before the United Nations, as well as answer anxious inquiries from our Ambassadors in foreign countries. Large numbers of telegrams were arriving from our embassies commenting on the situation in Northern Ireland and pointing out what harm it was doing to Britain's image. The Foreign Office complained to me, so although I had great sympathy with Chichester-Clark I had to remind him that the formal position was that the Foreign Office spoke for the UK in its dealings with Lynch and that this had been made clear in the Downing Street Declaration. Paragraph 2 of that

Declaration said that the UK Government would take full responsibility for Northern Ireland 'in all international relationships'.

A few days later Chichester-Clark wrote me a very pained letter
saying that he had not understood that he had entered into such an
obligation. He had thought the paragraph meant that the UK took
such responsibility in dealing with third countries or international
organizations but not as between North and South. He said that in
any case he had shown Oliver Wright what he had proposed to say
and had amended it in accordance with Wright's suggestions and
that his reply was meant to be helpful and constructive within the
limits of political realities. He had since discussed the matter with
his Cabinet and he hoped that we were not pressing for a requirement
that all such statements should be cleared in advance because this
would give rise to very great difficulties. If he could not speak quickly,
Craig and 'others of his ilk' would become the principal proponents
of the constitutional integrity of Northern Ireland. He said he would
certainly let us know as far ahead as possible of any statements he
proposed to make that might affect our relations with the South,
but he hoped he would not be inhibited from making a swift reply.

I thought that was a reasonable statement on his part so, trying to
keep the peace with the Foreign Office, I said I hoped we could handle
it in the same way as British Cabinet Ministers who, if they are
going to make a speech about another Minister's Department, are
expected to clear the text with that department first so that they
are aware of what is going to be said. Of course it is not always
possible to observe this procedure, especially if a Minister is asked
a question about foreign affairs at a meeting. He cannot pause and
tell the questioner that he must first telephone the Foreign Office
and clear his answer with them. I asked Chichester-Clark to do what
he could and pointed out that we were very fortunate in having
Oliver Wright in Belfast, because as a distinguished Foreign Office
official he would know the form and could communicate with them
quickly if he thought there were likely to be any international
repercussions. So this little irritation died down.

I took advantage of a speech to the Labour Party Conference in
Brighton at the end of September to call on the Catholics to make a
gesture of reconciliation towards the Protestant majority. It was not
the most popular line with a vocal minority of delegates, but the

great bulk of the Conference was with me. Anyway, I wanted to reassure the Protestants, knowing as I did then what Hunt would have to say about the police, and I am sure it was the right thing to do. I said I recognized that the Protestants had genuine and deeply felt fears too, and that so far it was they, through the reforms they had undertaken, who had made a gesture. 'The time is coming,' I went on, 'for the Catholics too to make their gesture towards assuaging the fears, however mistaken they may be thought to be, of the majority.' I said the Catholics could win more Protestant support for civil rights if they seemed to be willing to co-operate more in making the organs and apparatus of the Northern Ireland State work. In particular, I pointed out that if the Opposition, who were boycotting Stormont, were to return to their places, it would make the reforms easier for the Unionists to accept. I asked the Catholics to think again about their insistence on separate education, adding that I found it as offensive that separate education should be advanced as an unshakeable principle as that the group in power should deny a man a house because of his religion. I suggested that as a start sixth-form pupils from Catholic and Protestant schools might meet in order to get to know each other better. (Cardinal Conway's reaction to this specific suggestion was much milder than it might have been and I was grateful to him. He did not rule it out, and indeed described it as a 'reasonable idea'.) I also asked more Catholics to join the RUC, pointing out that whereas a third of the places in the force were reserved for Catholics, they had taken up only eleven per cent of them. Finally, I talked about the possibility of 'raising the whole Irish problem to a new plane'. By this I meant we had to look ahead beyond the short-term questions of securing civil rights and on to finding a new solution to the problem of the border, so that all in Ireland, North and South, could live together in peace and prosperity. I only hinted at this, saying it had to be approached with 'great care and great delicacy, but with great determination'. The remark was picked up and speculated on in the Irish Press, who saw what I had in mind, but not much was made of it in the British Press.

The day after I made my speech, Parliament reassembled at Stormont for a two-day debate on the Cameron Report. A representative of the Opposition MPs telephoned and told me they had decided to attend. The first day was marked by a vast and rowdy demonstration outside the Parliament buildings by about 5000 of Paisley's supporters, who jostled and jeered at MPs and attacked a number of reporters. Paisley said they had come to protest against the Cameron Report and show that they would resist any attempt to disband the B-Specials.

Chichester-Clark, meanwhile, was making a very helpful speech. He began by welcoming the attendance of the Opposition MPs, all of whom had turned up, and said that they now all had the chance of a fresh start. He accepted that the grievances which Cameron had found were justified and had to be remedied. He said they must govern with justice and generosity and try to deal with the root causes of fear and suspicion. He asked the House to endorse the programme of reform that was being put forward. At the same time Stormont gave a first reading to four important Bills: the Local Government Bill to establish a commission to recommend new boundaries; the Commissioner for Complaints Bill to appoint a commissioner to hear complaints against local and public bodies; the Community Relations Bill to establish a community relations commission; and the Electoral Law Bill to extend the local government franchise to include all people entitled to vote at Parliamentary elections, and to reduce the voting age to eighteen.

The day before I was to return to Northern Ireland, Quintin Hogg, who had been there on a brief visit prior to the Tory Party Conference, repeated in his trenchant way his complete support for our policies. 'I am backing Callaghan for all I am worth,' he said, adding, 'Any Unionist who thinks he will get a better deal out of me than out of Jim is an ass.' He made the same sort of remarks at the Conservative Conference, which was a very great help in cooling the situation, even if it did get him into some hot water with a few of his colleagues.

My visit began on the evening of October 8. It was almost six weeks to the day since I had first promised to return, but in other respects it was a most unfortunate date. First, I had an extremely heavy cold and cough and should have been in bed. Although the aircraft was pressurized, the flight left me quite deaf in one ear. Subsequently I had to have a lot of treatment for it and although it was only a minor matter, it did affect my physical well-being for a time. Second, and more importantly, I had arranged about nine months previously to open a new prison at Coldingley in Surrey on that day. It embodied an entirely new experiment in prison reform in Britain that I was extremely proud of, being designed to give every prisoner proper industrial training and an organized daily routine of interesting and useful work producing marketable goods, to be sold through commercial channels. As far as possible it was to operate like a normal factory floor. So I got the Press, the Trade Unions, employers and others interested and concerned and wanted to open it with an appropriate burst of publicity. In the event, however, the impact of it was smothered in the excitement over the Irish visit.

The first thing I said on arrival in Belfast was that now that measures to end discrimination were imminent there would have to be an end to 'this nonsense in the streets'. I had in mind that during the previous ten days there had been a number of outbursts of rioting, in response to which the Catholics had again erected their barricades, although these had subsequently been taken down. I regretted the phrase as soon as I had said it: it sounded so typically British, for I knew only too well that the troubles went far deeper than that. Next day most newspapers put the remark in quotation marks and I was very glad no more notice was taken of it.

Most of that day, October 9, was taken up in discussions with the Northern Ireland Cabinet on Lord Hunt's recommendations, which he had sent a few days earlier to Chichester-Clark. These were, briefly, that the RUC should be disarmed, relieved of its para-military duties and remodelled on the lines of other British police forces; that the B-Specials should be replaced by a part-time force under the control of the GOC Northern Ireland; and that a police authority should be set up composed numerically in proportion to the different groups within the community. Not surprisingly, the Northern Ireland Cabinet had had a lot of difficulties about these recommendations. They had discussed them on four separate occasions before I met them and I had had a number of telephone conversations with Chichester-Clark, sometimes two or three a day.

Their initial objections centred on the replacement of the B-Specials. Paragraph 171 (d) of the draft of the Hunt Report included the words 'disbandment of the Ulster Special Constabulary' and they wanted the word 'disbandment' to come out. It seemed a small concession to make if, with Hunt's consent, we could find a different form of words, as they felt so strongly about it. It was not difficult. The final Report eventually said that the new force would 'replace' the Ulster Special Constabulary: the meaning remained the same.

Next, they objected to paragraph 171 (a) which said that the new force would be 'under the command of the GOC'. They wanted the word 'operational' inserted before 'command'. This was very much more serious, and I told Chichester-Clark during one of our series of telephone conversations that the force must be controlled by Westminster and there could be no ambiguity about it. Chichester-Clark said that if the Northern Ireland Government had no control over it, he and his Cabinet would be bound to disagree with the Hunt Report. I said I was sorry to have to go over this ground again, but constitutionally there could be only one form of control over the armed forces of the United Kingdom and that was by the United Kingdom Parliament. This responsibility could not be shared and one part of the UK could not be permitted to run the Army. Consultation with the Northern Ireland Government was of course acceptable, but responsibility would have to lie at Westminster and nowhere else.

Chichester-Clark was very gloomy, but the next day he rang me and reported, to my great relief, that his Cabinet had moved from their position. However, they wanted assurances on six matters, which he then outlined. First, they wanted the British Government to agree to maintain the B-Specials until the new force, which they wanted to be called the Ulster Defence Regiment, had been created. I said straight away that I agreed to that: it had always been the intention. Second, there should be an immediate start on creating the new force, and I again gave the assurance that preparations were already in hand. Third, they wanted an assurance that the number of troops in Northern Ireland would always be adequate to meet emergencies. I said there need be no doubt about that, although of course I hoped for Northern Ireland's sake that it would not always have to be kept at the then level, which was about 8000. Fourth, they wanted an assurance that the Army would be available quickly on any future occasion. I said yes, but that I hoped after the new deal was fully implemented such an occasion would be unlikely to arise. Fifth, the Cabinet wanted me to make a statement at the end of my visit that action would be taken to resume police patrols in the no-go areas of Belfast and Londonderry. I said I wanted this as much as the Cabinet did. Sixth, they wanted an assurance that the Ulster Defence Regiment would not be disbanded except with the agreement of the Northern Ireland Government.

I was a little surprised at this and said, 'Surely you mean the Ulster Special Constabulary?' 'No,' he said, 'the Ulster Defence Regiment.' I said, 'Look, we have not raised the Force yet.' 'I know,' he said, 'but we are looking to the future and we want to make sure that it won't be disbanded without our agreement.' So I said, 'I don't think we can say this in public: it would create the wrong impression. Surely the Northern Ireland Government does not want anybody to think that the disbandment of the UDR is contemplated?' Chichester-Clark said he could see the difficulty in legislating about it but he did want an understanding between governments. I found no difficulty about that. I told him that we should certainly want their agreement if we were going to disband the UDR, although as always, of course, the final responsibility would lie with Westminster.

He then made one final request which, unbeknown to any of us, was to have serious consequences. We had originally planned to publish the Hunt Report on Thursday, October 9, the day of my arrival. My idea was that we could then publish the results of the working parties, set up during my previous visit, on the following day, Friday, and so keep up the momentum. But Chichester-Clark said it would be difficult to meet his Parliamentary Party on Thursday and he wanted to be able to rally them immediately the Report was published. So I agreed we should bring it out on Friday. If I had thought longer I might have reminded him that Friday is the start of the weekend and, with the drink flowing, it is always a bad time to announce anything controversial in Northern Ireland. But alas, I did not realize it then as poignantly as I did later.

Another subject we had discussed during those long telephone conversations before I left London was the successor to Peacocke as Inspector-General of the RUC. We both agreed that Peacocke would have to go – the Hunt Commission said in their Report that they believed their recommendations would call for 'outstanding qualities of leadership to carry them out' – and I wanted Sir Arthur Young, the City of London Police Commissioner, to take over.

Young had joined the police in Portsmouth at the age of eighteen and at thirty-one became the youngest Chief Constable in Britain. While he was Commissioner of the City of London Police he had been borrowed three times for important overseas missions, in the Gold Coast, Kenya and the Federation of Malaya, all of which not unnaturally earned him a reputation as a trouble-shooter. Field Marshal Sir Gerald Templer, who was our High Commissioner in Malaya, said when Sir Arthur left: 'He has been a real inspiration to the whole of the police. When he arrived they were somewhat dispirited. The situation is now different, due to his great drive and leadership.' I knew Young personally and he seemed to me to be exactly the right man for the job.

The idea of appointing him had come to me while I was attending the Labour Party Conference at Brighton and, telling no one what was in my mind because these things tend to go wrong if too many people know, I telephoned my Private Secretary at the Home Office and asked him to bring Young to see me urgently. I did not beat about the bush. I said to him, 'Arthur, I have got a difficult job for you to do and I don't want to take no for an answer.' 'What is this?' he asked. I told him. His one reply was, 'My God!' As I expected, he really did not want to go; he had a job to do in the City of London Police and wanted to get on with it. But I said, 'Arthur, it is your job to go, and you know you can do it, and very few other people can.' After a few minutes' talk he agreed. Chichester-Clark objected at first that Sir Arthur at sixty-one was too old and suggested two other names, both of whom were first-rate policemen in their own fields, but not, in my view, for Northern Ireland. Young was the man I wanted. He was a great personality and, I thought, a tremendous leader of men.

Since Chichester-Clark and I had been over the most controversial parts of the Report during our telephone conversations, there was not a great deal left to argue about when I met the Cabinet. None the less, in true Irish fashion we went through it all again. One of Hunt's most important recommendations was the establishment of a police authority. As I have mentioned earlier, it was extraordinary that the Inspector-General was responsible to no one for his operational functions, including para-military functions, and only to the Minister of Home Affairs, and thus to the Ulster Unionist Government direct, for all other policies. Of course, the Minister of Home Affairs could have dismissed him for failing to carry out his operational functions properly, but it would not have been proper for the Minister to direct him precisely. However, the minority claimed that the RUC was the armed wing of the Unionist Government.

Hunt dealt with the para-military aspect by recommending that these functions of the police – such as guarding the border – were properly the job of the armed forces of the crown and the police ought to be relieved of that responsibility. But this still left open the question of accountability. We have a very interesting system of accountability in this country whereby the police authority, composed of councillors and magistrates, can decide broad matters of policy but not question specific, individual actions. Thus if a motorist is prosecuted for exceeding the speed limit on a particular stretch of country road, the police authority is not entitled to question the Chief Constable about the individual prosecution. On the other hand, if there were a run of such prosecutions of motorists at the same spot, the police authority would be entitled to question the Chief Constable on his general policy in such a matter. Although this distinction is clearly understood on this side of the water, it was entirely unknown in Northern Ireland, and Hunt recommended that an Authority should be established whose members would be nominated by the county councils, the universities, the magistrates, the trades unions, Chambers of Commerce and others, and which would be responsible, among other things, for appointing the chief officer of police, his deputy and his assistant deputy officers. They would also have a particular duty to keep themselves informed about the way in which complaints against the police were dealt with.

The underlying theme of the Report was that policing in Northern Ireland should become more akin to policing in the UK. Hunt found that the RUC was cut off from the main stream of police activity in Britain, that it was isolated from the joint conferences and the central Inspectorate of Constabulary which, under the Home Office, link British police forces together. He recommended that the force should be inspected at least once a year by Her Majesty's Inspectorate of Constabulary. Another recommendation was that while the name of the force should not be changed, the RUC should exchange their dark green uniforms for the traditional blue. In the end this did not go through, mainly because, in the hurry to get the job done, a batch of second-hand blue uniforms were sent over. The men soon tumbled to this and naturally received them very badly indeed. I am afraid it was a detail that escaped me, and by the time the uniforms had been sent back and new ones had been tailored, Arthur Young had decided that the change would be more trouble than it was worth.

Hunt had an interesting observation to make on the extent to which Press and television coverage of events had resulted in magnifying the actual extent of the disorders and 'in generalizing the impression of misconduct by the police and of bad relations between the calm which has prevailed in most parts of Ulster, or the degree of deliberate provocation, the danger and strain under which the police, frequently and for long periods, tried to do their duty, as well as the fact that the great majority acted not only with courage but with restraint.' I think this was a fair criticism and it illustrated a difficulty that I found more than once while I was Home Secretary: the capacity of the media to magnify and therefore distort – perhaps not intentionally – the shape and significance of events.

The small screen can make quite minor happenings loom larger than life, and there are occasions, during demonstrations particularly, when the very presence of the television cameras whips up an insignificant handful of demonstrators who quickly realize that they are playing to several million viewers rather than to a group of bystanders. I remember one demonstration in London when the BBC transported to the scene a huge tower with cameras perched on top and blazing with lights. They were supposed to be reporting what was happening but their ostentatious presence enlarged the crowd, and encouraged the exhibitionists. They made the task of the police so difficult that eventually when shots were fired the superintendent in charge instructed his officers to shine their torches into the eye of the cameras. On that occasion, the Commissioner complained to me and I made sure Lord Hill knew about it. There were also occasions during night-time riots in Northern Ireland when the fury of the rioting visibly increased as soon as the cameras arrived and the powerful television lights were switched on. Later on, the television authorities, who were not unconscious of this, dealt with the matter by fitting their cameras with special lenses which enabled them to film at night by whatever light happened to be available. Throughout the whole period the question of the limits of the media's responsibility was a source of great worry to me.

The Cabinet having disposed of Hunt, we went on to discuss the reports of the joint working parties of civil servants which was the other chief task of my visit. Concentrating on the industrial and social problems that lay behind the more dramatic unrest on the streets, they had each of them done in six weeks a good six months' work. Throughout the period officials from the British and Northern Ireland Governments had been in constant contact with each other. First, they discussed the economy and the problems of attracting new investment and increasing employment. Quite a lot had been done between 1964 and 1968 for which not enough credit had been given. Thus new firms had been established at the rate of thirteen or fourteen a year and new jobs created at the rate of about 6500 a year. The volume of production in Northern Ireland during that time had increased by roughly three times as much as in Britain during the same period, while public investment in schools, roads, houses and so on had increase by 76 per cent. But the improvement was uneven, for Belfast was getting twice as many new jobs as the rest of the province put together, and the drift from the land of small farmers and farm workers was running at about 2000 a year. Unemployment in 1969, therefore, stood at about 28,000, 40 per cent of whom were men over the age of 45.

The working parties were surprised to find that the August disturbances had affected relatively few firms. Seventeen, employing about 1500 people, had had their production facilities destroyed but they all made a quick return to production. Their resourcefulness and resilience was quite remarkable. They were assisted financially by the Industrial Development Acts under which they received 70 per cent advances to purchase new machinery and 100 per cent advances to purchase new stock, the advances being made available immediately to be set off later against their compensation claims when these were finally settled. At that time the claims totalled about £16 million. The working party calculated that three new jobs had to be created in order to take one man off the unemployment register, because the creation of additional employment automatically reduced the migration rate to England and accelerated the movement off the land, since people reckoned that there would be more opportunities in the towns.

To meet this situation the working party discussed a series of proposals. One was a system of compensation for investors whereby if their premises were bombed or destroyed the Government would cover their reinstatement and any loss that they might suffer. They also proposed higher investment grants and a doubling of the winter relief work programme, including work on forestry and roads, which they estimated would employ 2500 people for between six and nine months. Helped by the advocacy of Jack Diamond, the Chief Secretary to the Treasury, my colleagues in the British Cabinet agreed all these proposals, so I was able to tell the Northern Ireland Cabinet that the Treasury was making available a contingent sum of £50 million under the compensation scheme – we hoped of course that very little of it would be needed – and a total of about £5 million to cover the increased investment grants and higher Selective Employment Tax repayments, together with a further £2 million for labour-intensive works. They greeted this news with considerable satisfaction.

Another important joint report was on housing needs. I had already received a study by the Ministry of Housing commenting very favourably on the work of the Northern Ireland Housing Trust, whose policies and standards, were far superior to those of the local authorities in Northern Ireland. The Trust, which was set up in 1945, owned about 41,000 houses and was building them at the rate of about 2000 a year. Of the 25 qualified housing managers in the province, 22 were employed by the Trust and two of the others had been trained by the Trust before they had gone to local authorities. The standard of local authority housing management was in general abysmal.

It was the Ministry of Housing's view that if the Trust's seven-man board was overhauled it would be able to take over the extra 76,000 houses owned by the local authorities, which was a step I had very much in mind. Housing, of course, was in a pretty bad state in Northern Ireland. About 150,000 houses, a third of the total stock, were over 80 years old. In the so-called Shankill redevelopment area, more than 90 per cent of the houses lacked inside water-closets, fixed baths and hot water systems, and these figures could be repeated for many other areas. It was this that led me to suggest to Chichester-

Clark later on that the whole of the Shankill and Falls Road area should be pulled down, gutted, and rebuilt at different ends of Belfast. I suggested that a verdant wooded park should be created in its place to be called the Chichester-Clark Park. Chichester-Clark rarely showed much reaction but this idea rather tickled him. He very sensibly said that he thought that it would create problems but that it was not impossible.

I had another report from a building design partnership which pointed out that there was practically no open space for the inhabitants of the central area, that it contained some 60,000 houses almost all of which had no more than 12 ft of frontage to the street. A quarter of the houses were overcrowded and a half of them were under-occupied. It was obviously an area ripe for root and branch redevelopment, and with bold imagination it could have been done. I asked Shirley Williams, who was Minister of State at the Home Office, to work on the notion, to discover what would be involved in rehousing, how much it would cost, how long it would take and where the new houses could be built. She did start work on it, but before she could get far the General Election came along and that was the last I ever heard of my proposal.

One of the results of these joint working parties was that Whitehall officials became enthusiastically involved in the affairs of Northern Ireland. Looking back now, it is hard to remember just how separate a country Northern Ireland used to be, although formally part of the UK. Most Members of Parliament knew less about it than we knew about our distant colonies, on the far side of the earth. It was, as I have said, a situation that had gradually developed over fifty years through the design of the Northern Ireland Government and the acquiescence of the UK Government, and when I consider the full extent of our intervention during the first few weeks against that background, I see no reason for any of those concerned to be ashamed of what they did.

We held two press conferences in Belfast on Friday, October 10. The first, in the morning was to present the Hunt Report and introduce Sir Arthur Young. Considerable anxiety lay behind that. At five o'clock that morning Arthur had been sitting at his desk in the City of London Police Headquarters waiting for a phone call to say that there was an RAF plane ready to fly him to Belfast.

When the phone did ring it was to say they were sorry but there was fog and they did not think they would be able to take off. Eventually the fog lifted in time for Arthur to arrive at the press conference just before it began, having come hot foot from Belfast airport.

It was the first time he and Chichester-Clark had met, and while the three of us were sitting in another room waiting for the reporters to assemble, Chichester-Clark, who was always extremely considerate, asked if I would like to join him at the conference. I said no, it was his responsibility, he was appointing a new Chief Constable. So he went in on his own, described to the Press what Hunt had reported and paid due tribute to Peacocke. During this time there was a vacant seat on his right-hand side. When he got to the point of announcing that Arthur Young was to be the new Chief Constable, a signal was given, Arthur strode in and showed he was in possession. This was exactly what I wanted. I cannot emphasize too often how little we could gauge the reactions of police or public to the swift changes, and I wanted Young properly installed and able to assume command in order to forestall any possible trouble. When a political initiative is planned, any politician worth his salt should be able to judge what reaction, if any, is likely. But in those early days in Belfast, I felt very often that I was steering by guess and by God.

Chichester-Clark then went to meet his Parliamentary Party, who after two and a half hours approved the Government's acceptance of the Report by 28 votes to 7 with two abstentions. Among those who voted against were Harry West, a former Minister of Agriculture, and Craig. Paisley denounced the proposals as a 'complete capitulation to the murderers and looters on the streets', but to counterbalance that extreme view it is worth recalling that they were welcomed by the Central Representative Body of the RUC. At a second, less dramatic press conference I announced the new industrial grants, the reconstruction programme and the creation of a new housing authority. I went on to say that the preceding days had been one of the most challenging and rewarding periods of my political life and I hoped that at the end of the day we should be able to see that some good had been done. 'This is not a last chance for Ulster,' I said, 'it is a great opportunity. Everyone in Ulster must face the fact that we are all children of God and everyone is entitled to and should receive an equal chance of a decent life.'

9

The following day, Saturday, I flew by helicopter to Londonderry where it was my chief, although until then secret, intention to take Sir Arthur Young, as the new head of the RUC, into the Bogside itself. I told nobody about this except my Private Secretary and Sir Arthur himself, of course. I don't intend to give the impression that I was only interested in cloak-and-dagger operations. Not at all. But employing the element of surprise and swiftness in a Northern Ireland situation gives less time for fears to be voiced, objections to build up and timorous advice to prevail.

Ostensibly the purpose of my visit was to meet an assembly of politicians, businessmen, trade unionists and other dignitaries at the Guildhall. It was a very informal occasion: we milled around talking and drinking coffee. Of those who were there I had confided only to John Hume that I wanted to visit the Bogside that morning, and even he did not know that I intended to take Sir Arthur behind the barricades. What I had asked him to do was to find me a house about 150 yards inside the Bogside where I could go and have another talk with the leaders without whipping up a great crowd. I did not want to risk the hurly-burly of the previous visit, although I knew from my experience in the terrace streets of my constituency in Cardiff how quickly news travels through such areas. I need only be in a Cardiff Street for two minutes when a little girl or boy will run up and say, 'Mr Callaghan, Mum says would you come down to see her at No. 57, she wants to have a word with you.' So too much advance publicity would have thwarted my plan.

Hume told me he had found a house belonging to an RAF corporal who was home on leave and who would be there with his wife. I asked him to go off and warn them I would be there in ten minutes and then turned to Young and told him that we were going to have to play it by ear. I must say he looked tremendously impressive: tall, massively broad, and wearing at my request his full uniform, complete with ribbons; I found him a most reassuring sight. I knew it would be useless to try to enter the Bogside alone with Arthur Young because at least 50 other people would be at our heels – the Press and television and officials and others following on from the Guildhall. So I got hold of the commanding officer and asked him to put a line of soldiers about 30-40 yards this side of the perimeter of the Bogside and to let only Young and myself through, stopping all the others. He agreed and left. When the time came to leave we got into the cars and I encouraged everyone else to climb in and told the Press, 'We are on our way now.' I did not tell them where I was going, as I knew they would try to follow. We set off as though on the next stage of our visit.

It was only about 150 yards from the Guildhall to the Bogside and I remember remarking to Arthur that we would have to move quickly because the soldiers would not be able to keep everybody back for very long. Then our driver suddenly changed course: we pulled up by the line of soldiers, and Young and I jumped out of each side of the car without formality and walked quickly to the perimeter of the Bogside across a sort of no-man's-land. The news had already begun to spread and there was quite a crowd waiting for us. As we marched across I said to him, 'Arthur, either you are going into the Bogside or we will both have a splendid funeral in Westminster Abbey.'

John Hume had arranged things well. He led us to the corporal's small terrace house and we sat down in the front room and were given a cup of tea. I introduced Young to the leaders of the Bogside community. A few minutes later the rest of our party came streaming through and once more the narrow street outside was jammed tight with people. Fortunately we were only a little way inside the Bogside and I did not have such doubts as before about getting through the crowd. Topper Brown, the Special Branch officer, had thoughtfully armed himself with a loud-hailer, with the others making a space for us outside the house. My message was basically this. 'Here is Sir Arthur Young, he is your new Chief Constable. I have brought him to you. You have got to look after him.' They responded to this approach and poor Arthur was slapped on the back unmercifully. Truth to tell, it did him a lot of good, and he played up and took the loud-hailer saying that he could only do his job if they helped him and he looked for their support.

After this we made our way through the crowd and went off to meet Commander Anderson, the Unionist MP, in the Protestant area on the other side of the city. As on the earlier visit, this was a more frosty gathering. Small knots of people were standing around on the street corner, some ready to pick a quarrel and to shout unfriendly remarks. Whenever this happened, I would walk over to whoever had shouted and try to engage them in conversation, picking up their phrases and asking, why do you say this? But it was not a great success. The conversations rapidly became incoherent because the people who were shouting were not the sort of people who intended to conduct a rational discussion. One woman yelled 'Lundy' in my ear, which in that part of the world means 'traitor', and another shouted 'The man who sold us to Rome', and someone else kept shouting 'Fenian lover', following me all down the street. It was a very useful reminder to me of the way in which some Protestant feeling was running, and it helped me to preserve a balance in my thinking. I realized that only a minority shouted abuse and that most of the people we passed either said good morning or stood quietly in their doorways, watching events. The majority of Protestants at that time were probably ready to give the changes a chance.

At the corner of a street we passed a gable-end wall of a house completely decorated with a larger than life painting of King William of Orange, and the artist, who was in a very excited condition, waylaid me to explain the significance of 1689 and would not let me go. As I was trying to introduce him to the realities of 1969 I was helplessly casting around for a way out of this situation when a woman started speaking to me. She was in real despair about the miserable housing conditions in which she lived and how she wanted a decent house. It was the kind of appeal I had heard many times in my own constituency in Cardiff and I recognized her genuine need. So I asked if she would show me where she lived. She said yes of course, and led me down a very narrow lane, no more than ten feet wide, which sloped so steeply that a rail had been erected down the middle to hold on to. The dwellings, to the best of my recollection, were neither two-storey nor one. Once inside the living-room which opened on to the lane, you went up a very narrow handful of stairs into a sort of attic-cum-bedroom. There was only the one living-room downstairs, and that was the extent of their home. She lived there with her husband and two children.

A crowd had gathered outside in the street by now and another woman said, 'Will you come and see how I live?' and I said, 'Of course I will. I want to see what is going on.' I went into two or three more houses, and now that the crowd could see I was really on the job the reception grew much calmer and friendlier. They said that no Member of Parliament had been into their homes for years and the fact that I was Home Secretary meant a lot to them. This was one of the personal experiences which reinforced the statistics of housing need and helped me to make up my mind that the housing programme in Northern Ireland had got to be stepped up even further. I remembered very well that the first woman who asked me to look at her house had said, 'I will live next door to anybody, Catholic or Protestant, if only I can have a decent house to bring the children up in.' It was the cry of the poor everywhere in the world.

In the afternoon we had a complete change of scene. After a quick lunch at HMS *Sea Eagle* my wife and I were driven along the wonderfully scenic coast road to the Giant's Causeway and then down through the glens of Antrim. It was a most enjoyable afternoon, only marred for me by the fact that I was still suffering from an extremely heavy cold and feeling dog-tired as a result. We were heading for Chichester-Clark's country home, Castledawson, where we had been invited for dinner. It is very much a country gentleman's residence, comfortable and obviously much cared for, full of dogs, guns and pictures. Attached to the house is a large farm, very efficiently run by Mrs Chichester-Clark, and I am sure it all made for a contented and satisfied life. I could quite understand why Chichester-Clark tried to get away from Belfast as often as he could. He had assembled a number of his neighbours and we had a very friendly and hospitable evening. During dinner he was called to the telephone and came back to tell me that there was trouble in Belfast. It was the first inkling we had of the horror to come, but the first information was that the rioting was being contained and that there was no need to worry unduly.

After dinner we returned to our hotel outside Belfast. At that time the disturbances were still not serious and my officials told me they would let me know if they got any worse. As my cold was still very heavy I was only too ready to retire to bed to get some sleep and, in truth, we were more worried then about the Bogside than Belfast. Joint Army and police patrols had been introduced into the Falls Road area two days previously and I had thought this an encouraging development. However, later that night serious trouble began.

It erupted not from the Catholics but from the Protestants, who were inflamed by the decision of the previous day to disband the B-Specials and disarm the RUC. As so often, it started in earnest after the pubs closed, at about the time I was getting back to my hotel. A large crowd gathered in Townsend Street at its junction with the Shankill Road. At first about 200 policemen armed with batons and riot shields tried to stop the mob, among whom were many drunks, from advancing down the Shankill towards the Catholic Unity Walk flats at the bottom. But the crowd, waving Union Jacks and singing Loyalist songs, hurled bottles and bricks at the police who retaliated with CS gas and linked arms across the street to stop the crowd's advance. The mêlée grew worse and suddenly a fusillade of shots rang out and Constable Victor Arbuckle, standing in the front line of the police, fell to the ground with a bullet in his head. He died almost immediately. The line was instantly restored unbroken. Two other policemen were injured by the same volley.

This was a signal for the Protestants higher up the road to throw up barricades of paving stones and overturned lorries from behind which came a hail of machine-gun bullets and sustained sniper fire. At 1.45 a.m. the troops opened fire in self-defence. These were the first shots they had fired since taking over eight weeks before.

So the bullets and the battle raged up and down the Shankill for the rest of that dreadful night, dying away only with first light on Sunday morning. By that time three people were dead, Constable Arbuckle and two civilians. Fourteen soldiers, three policemen and about 20 civilians were taken to hospital with gunshot wounds. Another 30 people were injured in other ways and 100 people were arrested.

I knew nothing about all this until I was woken very early on Sunday morning by Neil Cairncross and told of the events. He, like others of our team, had been up all night. I was angry at first at not being told earlier but Cairncross told me he had personally taken the decision not to disturb me, and on reflection I think he was right. Not only could I not have done much about what was happening, but more importantly, it meant that I was fresh and clear-headed to cope with the aftermath. I dressed quickly, found my driver and drove into Belfast to try to find who was in control. But there was nobody to be seen. The atmosphere was quite uncanny, like one Sunday morning I remember during the Blitz in London in 1941. We picked up Arthur Young and went to the police headquarters where a bleary-eyed and tired-looking man, who had obviously been on duty all night, unlocked the door to the Chief Constable's room. But it was obvious that I could not get a grip of the situation there; and the mob had gone home to sleep it off.

We then drove to the Army headquarters at Lisburn, where we found General Freeland in his office and there, as always, was action and coolness. We went over the situation together with a large-scale map in front of us and he told me that he was proposing to conduct a very rigorous search in the Shankill area that morning. He intended to cordon it off and use a helicopter to circle overhead, broadcasting to people that the Army intended to search their homes. I thought that some of the proposed steps would raise the temperature again and I urged him to use the utmost diplomacy. It seemed to me that the Army were in danger of over-reacting. Later, we went on to Stormont, where we found Faulkner, Porter and Chichester-Clark in a natural state of emotion. Chichester-Clark decided to make a lunchtime television broadcast about the events of the night. A draft had been prepared, but I thought it would have very little impact if he read it in that rather stolid way he has. I knew him to be a man of sincerity and, although he spoke with difficulty, when he did speak he did so shortly and well and you knew he was telling the truth. So I said to him, 'Why don't you try going on the air and just saying what you think instead of reading this beastly script?' In the light of what happened afterwards I am sorry to say he took my advice. I stood at his mantelshelf in front of a roaring fire and said, 'Now look, James, tell me what you feel about this situation.' And when he told me I said, 'All you need is four key words to remind you of what is in your mind as you go.' And I wrote down in big capital letters the four key words which I have since forgotten, and gave the foolscap sheet to him. He took it next door to the cameras. He only had to say about ten sentences altogether and these words would be his prompt. I told him to put himself over so that everybody could see what kind of a man he was. Alas, it simply was not in his nature, although he was none the worse for that.

Afterwards I felt I had let him down very badly especially when I read the Press comments, which suggested that the Prime Minister was so obviously ill that he must be on the point of resigning. However, he was so genuinely upset about everything just then that in the end it did not really matter.

I had meantime postponed my return to London for a day and cancelled an address I was due to have given on Sunday afternoon to a meeting of students at Queen's University. The theme of the conference, ironically enough, was to have been 'Community or Chaos'. That afternoon I wrote a letter of condolence to Constable Arbuckle's widow. He was twenty-nine, had two children, and had been in the force for eleven years. Later I was very grateful to get an understanding telephone call from Mrs Arbuckle's brother. Constable Arbuckle was the first victim of the attempt to build a non-sectarian society in Northern Ireland, and I shall not forget him.

The reforms themselves were scarcely revolutionary and did not warrant such a furious reaction. But in a real sense they undermined the dominant world the Protestants had inhabited for so long, a world of entirely different assumptions and objectives. The Protestants had settled ideas about the nature of their society and their ascendancy over the minority, and felt this was all cut from under their feet by the changed role of the police. Psychologically, it was a very traumatic experience for them, and I tried to understand this. Whether we gave sufficient weight to it is something that others will judge. It seemed to me essential that as Northern Ireland was a part of the UK we should try to create the kind of structure there that we had in the rest of these islands and we were demanding no more of the Protestants than they ought to have been ready to give. But they did suffer from the lack of a clear lead from above which would have made them feel that their interests were being guarded. Paisley could have done it. So might Craig. Chichester-Clark, who had no charisma despite his other qualities, was never really capable of giving it.

Though I doubt whether even if there had been a different kind of leadership we could have escaped the events of that weekend.

Of course we ought to have been better prepared for the reaction. The size of the Protestant crowd that night was about 3000 and there were only 200 policemen there to control them. It emphasizes a point I have made before: if the Metropolitan Police had been involved they would have been present in overwhelming strength. The mob would have thought twice before challenging them, and if they had been challenged, the police would have been strong enough to contain them. Despite the shortage of police, during the next six months, up to Easter 1970, there was not a single serious outbreak of violence. That is very significant in my opinion and justifies our policies. They succeeded at the cost of the death of one policeman, and the situation from then on improved week by week.

The following week, for example, the RUC patrols went back first into the Falls Road area of Belfast and then into the Bogside in Londonderry. They were unarmed but backed up by troops in case there should be any resistance, which there was not. Arthur Young ran into trouble with his men in Belfast and when he asked for volunteers to go into the Falls Road only one young policewoman came forward. There was a certain amount of shuffling among the men at this, and in the end, the first patrol that went in comprised two policewomen and District Inspector Frank Lagan, a very brave man who had been kicked to the ground during a riot the previous April. These three walked up the Falls Road and stopped and spoke to Jim Sullivan, Chairman of the Citizens' Defence Committee and a known IRA man. He told the Press later that he would never have welcomed the police under the previous Inspector-General but believed that the reformed RUC under Arthur Young would bring a return to normality. Lagan was asked what he felt about having been attacked in the rioting and he replied in a very generous way that bygones should be bygones, and that seemed to be the attitude of the Falls Road too. The policemen who had declined to volunteer for the patrol were worried about being asked to go into the Falls Road after dark to make an arrest without weapons. They were in favour of becoming an unarmed civilian force and said so, but they wanted their arms phased out over a period in night-time patrols. Arthur Young kept this fear very much in mind and at first the patrols only went in during the day.

A few days later it was the turn of Londonderry, and the RUC went back into the Bogside. The first two constables, who were accompanied by Military Police, were cheered by a small crowd of onlookers as they crossed the white line which had been painted across the road to mark the boundary of so-called Free Derry. There were a few jeers from a group of youths, but the adults remonstrated with them and so the police were generally welcomed.

The next weekend Arthur Young toured the Protestant and Catholic areas of Belfast, talking to people, showing himself – he had a splendid sense of what was required – and the police said afterwards that it was the quietest weekend since the troubles began, by contrast with the previous weekend which had been the most violent for some years. Robert Porter, the Minister of Home Affairs, very sensibly introduced a drinks curfew in Belfast that weekend which shut down all the city's 600 public houses at 7 p.m. The curfew was so successful that it was repeated on succeeding weekends, which remained quiet.

When I left Belfast on the morning of Monday, October 13, it was with a sense that much had been accomplished in the previous six weeks. Our promise to take a new initiative and make a fresh start had been kept and we had created within that short time a comprehensive programme of reform for Northern Ireland. Apart from the Hunt Report, which was obviously vital to our plans, I attached a great deal of importance to the creation of the central housing authority. Inadequate housing, and allocation according to religious belief by a small number of local authorities, had long been a cause of justified complaint. The new housing authority would take responsibilities away from the local authorities and was a momentous change. Faulkner, the Minister responsible, agreed with it and was most helpful in persuading his Cabinet colleagues to go along with it.

I reached London at midday and immediately had to plunge into opening a debate in the Commons at 3.30 p.m. in the afternoon. This does illustrate the kind of life Ministers lead, which puts a very great strain on them. In the previous fourteen days I had spent the first week at the Party Conference, going to long and involved meetings of the National Executive Committee, sitting through the Party Conference itself, making a speech on Northern Ireland, going to numerous social functions in the evenings, seeing Arthur Young, keeping the Home Office business going while I was away, remaining in constant telephone touch with Chichester-Clark. Then, when I returned to London, I had to catch up on many aspects of Home Office business, attend Cabinet and other meetings, before leaving for four very tense days in Northern Ireland. One carries it through at the time but there is a reaction afterwards. Anyway on that Monday afternoon I gave the House a recital of what had been achieved, and still had to be achieved, and made a strong attack on Paisley whom I accused of using the language of war cast in a biblical mould. I said that 'Fight the Good Fight' sung in a peaceful English village church on a Sunday morning sounded very differently when it was sung in the Shankill Road after a night of rioting.

10

It was at about this time that the position of the Governor, Lord Grey, began to trouble us. He lived, not by his desire, in somewhat faded splendour at a mansion at Hillsborough, outside Belfast, but although he was required to live there, he did not receive sufficient emoluments to enable him to maintain the dignity of a constitutional monarch – my phrase, not his. But was he a constitutional monarch?

The difficulty first arose when we were considering the possibility of suspending Stormont. Lord Grey pointed out that the constitutional facts had become conveniently obscured and that his predecessors had come to regard themselves as the constitutional representatives of a constitutional sovereign who acted on the advice of their local Ministers. Broadly speaking, the constitutional position was that he stood in the position of the sovereign in the administration of the transferred services. But during the twenty-five-year reign of one of his predecessors, the Duke of Abercorn, the evolution of affairs lent some colouring to the notion that even on other matters he acted more like the Governor-General of an independent country within the Commonwealth than the Governor of a dependent territory, responsible to the United Kingdom at Westminster. None the less, Lord Grey, according to his Letters Patent – his royal instructions – dated November 24, 1964, was required, among other things, to withhold assent to Northern Ireland Bills if so instructed by the Sovereign, which meant the Government at Westminster. He was also authorized to exercise the power of pardon; and he was not entitled to swear anyone who was not a minister into the Privy Council of Northern Ireland without having first obtained approval from the Britsh Home Secretary. So in these respects it was clear that he was subject to direction from Westminster and was not a Governor-General acting on the advice of his local Ministers. Lord Grey correctly reminded me, on the other hand, that when he was

129

appointed I told him to regard himself as Terence O'Neill's man – by which I meant the Northern Ireland Prime Minister's man – rather than the representative of Westminster. In other words, like so much else in Northern Ireland, it was a cat's cradle due to neglect by Westminster over the years and the encroachment of the Northern Ireland Government.

After the troubles of September and October Lord Grey felt that it had become important that he should be the focus of representation of the UK Government in the province. If that was to be the case, he argued, he would need more staff and other facilities; besides, the value of money had declined and his representational activity had fallen below the standard that he would like. He pressed us for an early answer on all this, which, frankly, I was not ready to give.

During this period we reviewed the much neglected Section 75 of the Government of Ireland Act 1920 which laid down that the supreme authority of the Parliament of the United Kingdom 'shall remain unaffected and undiminished'. Other parts of the Act, which forms Northern Ireland's constitution, were also significant. For example Section 6 (1) says that the Northern Ireland Parliament shall not have the power to alter or repeal any part of the Government of Ireland Act. Section 6 (2) was also clear. It said that where any Act of the Northern Ireland Parliament deals with any matter also dealt with by any Act of the UK Parliament the Act of the Northern Ireland Parliament should be read subject to the Act of the UK Parliament, and so far as it is repugnant to that Act shall be void. In other words, in the case of a conflict of laws it is quite clearly laid down that Westminster shall prevail. Section 22 makes clear that the imposition and collection of income tax, customs duties and corporation profits tax are all powers reserved to Westminster and that the proceeds of those duties and taxes should be paid into the consolidated funds of the UK. So Northern Ireland was in no way an independent territory, although we had the difficulty of changing habits of mind under which by convention it had come to regard itself as such.

Much of this *laissez-faire* attitude derived from a decision made by the Judicial Committee of the Privy Council as long ago as 1924. The treaty of 1921 which partitioned Ireland and established the Irish Free State in the south provided for a boundary commission to determine the border between North and South. The commission was to comprise one member appointed by the Northern Ireland Government, one appointed by the Free State Government and the third by the British Government. However, the Northern Ireland Government declined to make such an appointment and the Privy Council was asked to decide whether 'it is competent for the Crown, acting on the advice of Ministers of the UK, to instruct the Governor of Northern Ireland in default of advice from his Ministers to make an appointment and for the Governor of Northern Ireland to act upon that instruction.' As a layman, I would have thought that was pretty clearly covered by Section 75 of the Act of 1920. But the Privy Council gave an answer in the negative. They said: 'The appointment is not committed to the Governor, who only acts in this matter as the mouthpiece of his Minsters responsible to Parliament.' From that judgment it was a short slide into the position that the Governor was wholly responsible to Northern Ireland Ministers, and step by step the British Government withdrew. British Conservative Ministers were not very anxious to intervene against their Ulster Unionist friends and the Privy Council's ruling gave them a valid excuse not to do so. Forty-four years later, in the winter of 1968, we drafted a 'take-over' Bill, based on the provision of Section 75 that Westminster enjoyed the paramount legislative power and by that means we by-passed any constitutional confusion over the Governor's position.

Towards the end of 1969, as week followed week without serious trouble, the atmosphere in the Home Office became much more relaxed and the Civil Service was able to give some long-term thought to the future. A very powerful committee examined these constitutional problems and, as is their custom, once they had reached their conclusions they drafted a memorandum for me to submit to the Cabinet, if I agreed. They proposed that, in the event of a take-over, executive power should be concentrated in the hands of a Governor, and not be given to a Minister. This was similar to Lord Grey's own suggestions and I do not think they were surprised when I said I disagreed. I wrote that in the event of a take-over while I was at the Home Office I would prefer an executive Minister to be resident in Northern Ireland who would not be a policy-making Minister but would act under my general guidance and advice. I wanted to keep the problem in my own hands. In the end I did not submit their painstaking memorandum to the Cabinet and it is interesting that the Conservative Government has reached similar conclusions, for their take-over legislation in March 1972 gave the necessary powers to a British Minister and not to the Governor, although the office has now been separated from the responsibilities of the Home Secretary and William Whitelaw is, of course, a full Cabinet Minister.

One of the most important pieces of legislation I had to handle in the winter of 1969 was the Police Act 1970 which was designed to convert the RUC into a British-type police force in such matters as standards of efficiency and methods of policing. One of the most important provisions was for an interchange between members of the RUC and British police forces and for British policemen to assist the RUC if they required it. We made the exchange process operate both ways if necessary, but it was in our minds that the RUC was hardly likely to be called upon to assist the British police. However, the Act enshrined the principle of interchangeability and equality. I did not have much trouble getting in the agreement of the House of Commons to the Act but various organizations raised detailed objections to it. The Association of Municipal Corporations and the County Councils Association saw it as the first step towards a national police force in the United Kingdom, which of course it was not. They argued that if the Home Secretary could direct the chief officer of a police force to give assistance to the RUC this strengthened the control of the Home Office over the police at the expense of the local police authorities. In a sense it did, although that was not the purpose. Fortunately the momentum of events and the overwhelming support I had for the proposals was such that they did not pursue their objections very far. I gave an undertaking to Parliament that no exchanges would take place until conditions in Northern Ireland approximated to conditions in Britain in the matter of policing. This was to meet the doubts of the Police Federation which did not want the British police to operate the Special Powers Act.

The moment to test the water had come, I thought, when we began discussing how we would cope with the big Orange parades that were to take place all over Northern Ireland in late June and early July 1970. Early in June we arranged for Robert Porter, the Minister of

Home Affairs, to send us a formal request for the short-term loan of 1500 British policemen. This would have meant a substantial increase in the effective strength of the RUC for the short period of the week-end marches. We would have got closer to the basic British police philosophy of saturating a potential trouble area as the best means of stopping trouble before it starts. In his letter to me Porter said that to overcome any difficulty in meeting his request, he gave an under-taking that the British police would not be required to operate the Special Powers regulations. This was what I needed. I had let the impression be given that I was not keen to ask for British police to go to Northern Ireland because I knew the British police would object to operating the Special Powers Act, but Porter's assurance would now meet their objections. Porter also said that the British police would not be used in the Falls or the Shankill or in Londonderry: his intention was that they should line routes intermingled with the RUC in what were regarded as safe areas and in Belfast particularly. Sir John Waldron, Commissioner of the Metropolitan Police, told me he was ready to comply but was firm that the Metropolitan police must work under their own officers and not under the RUC and that they must operate separately from the Army. He wanted them to take charge of a complete area and operate on their own. We also decided to draw policemen from the Lancashire and the Yorkshire forces and I asked the officials at the Home Office to talk the matter over with the Police Federation because their co-operation was essential. That was as far as our plans had got by June 18, 1970 when we left office, and it was the last I ever heard of the plan.

We had announced our detailed proposals for raising the Ulster Defence Regiment, which was to replace the B-Specials, in a White Paper in November 1969. It was to be under Whitehall's control, have a maximum strength of 6000 – it was later raised to 10,000 – and be modelled on the Territorial Army. It would cost about £1 million a year. The basic principles were that the force would be part of the British Army, be subject to military discipline, open to all citizens, and it would not be used for riot control. Objections were raised to the name of the regiment on the ground that the traditional province of Ulster comprised nine counties and not the existing six, and that the name was therefore 'offensive' to Catholics. I was slightly shaken when Lord Hunt, speaking in a debate in the Lords, took the same line, but the overwhelming majority of *both* Parties were in favour of the proposed title.

During the passage of the Bill, Michael Foot accused me of having done a deal with Stormont which made it impossible for the British Government to accept any amendments to the Bill establishing the regiment. This was partly true. I had done a deal in the sense that I had entered into an open agreement with Stormont on the terms and conditions for raising the regiment. What was untrue was that the deal was a secret or sordid one. I pointed out to my critics that I had made a series of agreements with Stormont on a wide range of reforms, of which the UDR was part, and that if we started to break our side of the bargain it was going to be that much more difficult to ask the Northern Ireland Government to keep theirs, and I might have added that I was not then either ready or anxious to take over the Administration. Recruiting for the regiment opened on January 1, 1970, and the first two applicants were Catholics. By April, when 1800 men had enrolled, 20 per cent of the recruits were Catholics, which was much better than many people had feared. It was sufficient to show that the UDR was not just the B-Specials under another name.

By the middle of November Northern Ireland had had its quietest four weeks since the troubles began. The weekend curfew on the pubs was lifted and the Press reported a cautious optimism among Government Ministers and the security authorities. Sir Arthur Young announced that there were no areas in Northern Ireland where the RUC could not go, and the Army, at the end of its first 100 days' operation in the province, swung into what it called a 'hearts and minds offensive'. The troops organized a meals-on-wheels service for old people in Londonderry, took youths from Belfast climbing in the Black Mountains, organized dances and so on. As Christmas approached, the flood of invitations to individual soldiers became almost embarrassing. One senior officer described the inhabitants in his area of Belfast as 'the nicest, friendliest, most hospitable and sometimes most maddening people in the world', which I thought summed it up rather well. None the less, the Army let it be known that they expected troops would have to stay in Northern Ireland for at least another three years and probably longer. One cloud on the horizon was the six-month prison sentence

imposed on Bernadette Devlin for her part in the Londonderry riots
the previous August. This provoked some Catholic rumblings but
she appealed against conviction and so the reaction was postponed.

Despite the official sigh of relief, however, the peace in Belfast
between the communities was never more than precarious and on
five successive nights at the end of January, angry, chanting crowds
of Protestants roamed up and down the Shankill threatening the
Catholic Unity Walk flats and the Army peace line between the
Shankill and the Falls Road. The excuse for their protest was the
failure of the authorities to introduce full (as opposed to modified)
police patrols in the Catholic areas. The Catholics, on the other
hand, felt that many of their basic grievances remained and were
further upset by Arthur Young's decision not to discipline sixteen
policemen accused of misconduct in Londonderry the previous
January. The charges ranged from drinking on duty to throwing
stones.

Then, during February, there was a series of explosions in the
province which were attributed to, and sometimes acknowledged by,
the Ulster Protestant Volunteers. Until Easter, however, Belfast
remained relatively quiet, but over the Easter weekend there was an
outburst of vicious rioting in Ballymurphy, a Catholic estate on the
slopes of the hills above Belfast. In two nights of disturbances more
than 100 petrol bombs were thrown at troops, who replied with CS
gas, and General Freeland issued a warning that anyone carrying
or throwing petrol bombs was liable to be shot dead after a warning.

We did not know it at the time, but those riots marked the
emergence of the Provisional IRA as a separate force. The split
within the Republican movement had come into the open at their
annual conference three months earlier. Then the trench-coated
traditionalists – 104 of them in all – had walked out and formed what
they called the Provisional Army Council after a majority of the 260
delegates present had taken the unprecedented step of voting in
favour of resolutions committing the movement to recognizing the
Parliaments in Belfast and Dublin – and working for the ideal of a
socialist workers' republic. The IRA and its political wing, Sinn Fein,
had been moving steadily to the left since 1965, abandoning the
gun and the bomb and concentrating on political and social issues
in the South as well as the North. The result, according to the

disaffected Provisionals, was that in August 1969 the Catholics of Belfast and Londonderry had been unarmed, untrained and un-protected from the Protestant extremists. Now the Provisionals used Easter to make their bid for popular Catholic support by exploiting their fears and grievances. Gerry Fitt, who had done so much to draw the attention of Westminster and of the world to the injustices suffered by the Catholics, described the rioting as a personal tragedy for his methods. 'The heart has been knocked out of me,' he told me. Four weeks later the great gun-running scandal hit Dublin. Two of Mr Lynch's senior Ministers, Charles Haughey and Neil Blaney, were dismissed after allegations that they had been involved in an attempt to smuggle guns destined for the IRA in the North.

All this, of course, led to increased tension in Belfast and renewed outbreaks of violence. In this atmosphere Paisley had been elected to Stormont by defeating the official Unionist candidate in a stirring by-election at Bannside, the seat held by O'Neill until he accepted a peerage. This result strengthened the extremists on both sides and Chichester-Clark acknowledged that his party was now split three ways, between Paisley's Protestant Unionists, the liberal Unionists, and those who supported the official Unionist cause. Chichester-Clark himself suffered a setback when he was replaced as vice-chairman of his own Unionist branch at Castledawson by a local bus driver.

I received reports at the end of April 1970 that the right wing was gaining ascendancy in the Unionist Party and that Chichester-Clark was nearing the end of his tether and might very well be defeated or resign. It was thought that if Chichester-Clark did go we should have to consider suspending the constitution. My reply to this was that I would return to Northern Ireland fairly soon to see what was to be done, and in the meanwhile if Chichester-Clark did drift to the right or was forced to resign, I should not hesitate to introduce direct rule and that I was not bluffing about it. Our sources of information were much improved and I had received a report from Sir Arthur Young in April to the effect that if the British Government had to take over, the men of the RUC could be relied upon to support it. This was encouraging and gave me a freer hand.

By this time I knew that the British General Election was soon to be held and I felt we had to get past that if I was to have the necessary authority to take drastic new steps. My intention was to call a round-table conference to try to devise some new constitutional settlement. It must be remembered that despite the unrest we were still operating against a background of relative peace and quiet and a constitutional conference in that atmosphere would have stood a much better chance of success than one called after hundreds of murders and shootings and explosions. During that relatively quiet period I was looking ahead, preparing for the next steps, for I knew that we could not sit back and rely on the reform programme to solve all our problems. This was to be Maudling's mistake when he became Home Secretary.

Chichester-Clark came to see me for the last time before the Election on May 13. His chief purpose was to discuss a big new five-year Development Programme for Northern Ireland, which we had been preparing following the reports of the working parties in the previous autumn, and which we wished to launch quickly. The Programme involved a substantial expenditure for econmic and social development and I was able to tell him what he was anxious to know: that the expenditure had all been agreed by the Treasury and an announcement could be expected soon. In the event it was held up until after the Election.

The basis of the Programme was a Report by three consultants, Professor Sir Robert Matthew, Professor Thomas Wilson and Professor Jack Parkinson, who had been appointed by the Northern Ireland Government in 1968. It was not very exciting work and did not catch the headlines, but it was extremely valuable. I thought, however, that it was variable in its assessment: some things the consultants did very well, other issues I found unconvincing. Although it was a report to the Northern Ireland Government, many of its recommendations had to be cleared with the UK Government because it was the British Treasury that would have to pay for them. Northern Ireland finances only about 80 per cent of its requirements. Whether the balance should be called a subsidy is a matter of argument, but Northern Ireland's position in this is no different from Scotland's or Wales's or indeed any other region, and it is part of the ethos of the UK that Parliament should consider the kingdom as a whole. In any case, I was not content to be just a postman and transmit to the Cabinet the requests of the Northern Ireland Government made on the basis of the consultants' report, and at a fairly early stage I asked J. M. W. 'Michael' Stewart, a young economist, to assess the report for me. Stewart had served in the Department of Economic Affairs and then gone to Zambia to assist the Government there with their development plan.

I was later to find out that as early as January 1969, before the troubles came to a head, the consultants had submitted a statement to the Northern Ireland Government saying they viewed political developments at that time with deep concern, pointing out that these greatly increased the difficulty of attracting new industry to the province. They went on: 'We would therefore respectfully urge that further reform is needed, or a definite commitment that such reform will be adopted as a matter of urgency, otherwise one must express some doubt about the usefulness of proceeding in these circumstances with the work on a new development programme.' They repeated their warning to the Cabinet in May 1969, but, of course we knew nothing of this advice at the time.

A significant part of their report dealt with the inadequacy of housing and planning in Belfast. In a polite manner they confirmed what all of us who had had any dealing with the City Council knew from practical experience, namely that the city authorities had fallen down on the job. The consultants proposed a plan for the redevelopment of Belfast which encouraged me in my thinking about the need to empty the centre of the city – a move which I believed would be quite effective in reducing tension between the communities. The consultants said the growth of population in the centre was getting out of hand and that there was a need for a massive rehousing programme. Something else that fitted into my own thoughts was their recommendation for a new central housing authority to take the place of the numerous existing housing authorities. It was something I favoured for political reasons, and their report gave me a firm foothold.

Much of their analysis and recommendations were good, but they were at fault in allowing themselves to be seduced by the trendy economic thinking that investment grants to industry had little value. The Conservative Party were taking the line that our changeover in 1966 from a system of tax allowances to investment grants was unselective, undiscriminatory and meant that the State was not getting value for money. I am afraid the consultants swallowed this view and said that so far as increasing employment was concerned, they had 'some difficulty in recommending an appropriate course of action to the Government of Northern Ireland because the root of the trouble in our view is that the whole system of industrial grants in the United Kingdom is open to criticism and needs to be modified.' This was very unfortunate because the new Conservative Government, having come to power, in 1970, abolished investment grants at a stroke, only to reintroduce them again under a different name eighteen months later, as the most effective means of encouraging new investment. The Labour Government's policy was retrospectively justified, but meantime industrial development suffered in Northern Ireland, as elsewhere.

Equally unfortunately, the consultants also opposed the Regional Employment Premium that we had introduced, on the grounds that the cost was large when measured against the probable benefits and the Premium would further distort the wage structure. In this too, they were in line with some short-sighted thinking by the Tory Party. What they failed to see was that the distortion of the wage structure in favour of the development areas was the major purpose of giving a subsidy to wages: it was equivalent to a regional devaluation of sterling, and therefore lowered the costs of Northern Ireland, and made their products that much more competitive. However, they did report favourably on the Industrial Development Act, another measure of the Labour Government's, which helped new industry.

Michael Stewart's task was to prepare a critique of the consultants' economic analysis for my use. He found that Northern Ireland's unemployment problem was not unique and could be found in some regions of most advanced industrial countries, especially those furthest from the political, economic and cultural centres of power. He pointed out that a common feature of those regions was a heavy reliance on outdated industry – in Northern Ireland's case agriculture, linen, textiles and shipbuilding – and an ageing and inadequate infra-structure, which was especially true of Northern Ireland's housing. In such circumstances emigration was often put forward as a solution but he did not think we should rely upon that. He said that the consultants' proposals for creating additional employment were not satisfactory and went on to suggest the setting up of a development corporation. Such a scheme would take a considerable time to get under way but he thought it ought to be examined urgently. He also recommended that more financial assistance should be given to the private sector to encourage it to invest in Northern Ireland, and he suggested it might be offered price preferences in Government contracts. It was his view – very much in line with my own thinking, I may say – that labour costs should be subsidized more heavily. The argument against this is that it encourages employers to use labour wastefully, but there is little economic sense in that proposition until labour becomes a scarce factor of production. Another objection to subsidizing labour was that it did not encourage the establishment of modern growth industries. Stewart's comment was that if such industries were labour intensive the argument was simply not true, and if they were not labour intensive but used a lot of capital in relation to labour, the contribution they could make to the unemployment problem was limited, particularly in a depressed area where a large proportion of those out of work tend to be old or unskilled or both. Another argument used against subsidizing labour was that it was already cheaper in the depressed areas than the rest of the country and so further subsidy did not seem to be effective. Stewart's reply was that labour might be cheaper but it still was not cheap enough to offset the disadvantages of employing it in Northern Ireland, measured against low productivity, higher transport costs and fewer external economies. He said that the real reason for the current bias in favour of subsidizing capital rather than labour was that subsidies to capital were regarded as more respectable and less detectable than subsidies to labour. All capital investment in all countries was subsidized in the sense that tax allowances were permitted against depreciation on the investment. Subsidies to capital which involved improving those allowances were much more acceptable to business, and especially big business, than an overt subsidy to their labour force.

The basic conclusion of Stewart's report was that since the export of goods – mainly to Britain – accounted for some 80 per cent of Northern Ireland's gross domestic product, the logical way of creating more manufacturing employment was to reduce the price of those goods in relation to Britain by giving them a disguised devaluation. This, incidentally, coupled with a separate currency, would be the best way of making a unilateral declaration of independence work, provided Britain did not put up tariff barriers in retaliation. Stewart argued strongly in favour of increasing the Regional Employment Premium, which he suggested should be doubled at a cost of between £12 million and £15 million a year. Given the nature of the problem we had to deal with, this did not seem at all an excessive figure. Stewart thought it might mean between 15,000 and 20,000 more jobs being created over five years.

An additional attraction for me was that paying a Regional Employment Premium tends to prevent industry being footloose, whereas tax allowances and capital grants encourage an industry to go to a place for three or four years to reap all the fiscal and other advantages and then, if things are not going too well, they move out. Payment of part of the wage costs, on the other hand, gives industry a very powerful incentive to stay because they cannot take labour with them if they leave. A disadvantage of REP at the time was that the Conservatives had succeeded in undermining the confidence of businessmen in its continuance with their repeated attacks on its efficacy, and despite appeals they confirmed that it would be removed in 1974. Too bad for Northern Ireland, Scotland, Wales and the distant regions of England. As a whole, Michael Stewart's document fitted in well with my practical observation of the development area in South Wales with which I was acquainted, and I found it very valuable in my discussions with the Treasury.

The pros and cons for holding the General Election when we did are complex, and this is not the place to go into them, except to say that if we had won, as we were generally expected to do, it would have greatly strengthened our authority in Northern Ireland. So I was in favour of fighting the Election and getting it over with – although not for that reason alone. Northern Ireland continued to take up a great deal of my time while the campaign was on. My wife and I undertook an enjoyable but exhausting tour up through Wales and the North and then back through the Midlands and Reading to South Wales. It was a very hot summer and we had to face long drives from town to town, followed by crowded meetings, hecklers, and messages from the Home Office waiting for me at various stops. I had decided before the Election to use the facilities of the Welsh Office in Cardiff, where my friend, George Thomas, Secretary of

State for Wales, kindly set aside a suite for my use so that I could set up an office and staff it. We had a direct communications link with Whitehall and virtually took the major decisions of the Home Office from Cardiff itself. My habit was to rise early in the morning and begin the day with a long telephone call to Transport House to discuss election tactics. Then to the Welsh Office for an hour or two to deal with urgent matters that had arisen. Cardiff is such a compact city that I could then spend the rest of the morning canvassing in my constituency. This would be followed by a visit to a works canteen for lunch and a short speech, and then there would be more canvassing in the afternoon. At five o'clock I would go back to the Welsh Office, catch up on the paper work, return home for an hour for a meal and rest, and then address two or three meetings in the evening. All in all it was a hectic time.

Alas, the result of the General Election, when it came, was a disaster for Northern Ireland. Not only were the initiatives we had intended not followed up, but the break in continuity came at the very worst time for the success of the struggle to prevent the Provisional IRA from capturing the sympathy of the minority.

11

After June 18, 1970, my first-hand knowledge of events as a Minister came to an end. However, I continued as spokesman for the Labour Party on Northern Ireland matters until the end of December 1971, and remained very closely in touch with developments up to that time.

The election of Mr Heath's government brought rejoicing to the extreme Protestants, although less violent partisans realized that it could mean considerable difficulties ahead. The extremists had been disappointed by Quintin Hogg's unswerving support of the Labour Government's policies during the preceding eighteen months and this may have contributed to the incoming Prime Minister's decision not to offer Quintin the post of Home Secretary which he so much wanted. On the day after the election Quintin telephoned me at home, and by the way he spoke I assumed that he was to be appointed Home Secretary, although no official announcement had been made. He asked for my views on the situation and I brought him up to date as far as I could and also outlined some of the questions he would need to deal with immediately. These included the series of Protestant marches due to start on June 27, only nine days later. Should they be banned, or, if they were permitted to go ahead, should they be re-routed away from the Catholic areas?

Another important question was whether the Army or the RUC should take control of the marches, or whether their spheres of operations should be entirely separate. This was a recurring cause of friction between Sir Arthur Young and General Freeland. Another question was whether British policemen should be sent to Northern Ireland to take charge of an area during the marches, and if so, where it should be and under whose control they should operate.

I outlined some of these things to Quintin Hogg and so was surprised when the names of the Ministers were announced to see that Reginald Maudling had been appointed Home Secretary. I

143

was disappointed for Quintin; despite his aberrations, he is a great libertarian and would have made a good Home Secretary. However, Reginald Maudling had plenty of common sense and an outstanding intelligence and I thought that this would see him through.

Maudling did not approach me about the problems of Northern Ireland. In fact, our only conversation in the early days took place as we marched side by side from the Commons to the House of Lords to hear the Queen's speech at the opening of Parliament. A ceremonial procession was hardly the place for a detailed discussion. He said he intended to continue the policy that I had followed and that he felt it necessary to leave a lot of responsibility to the men on the spot. This last was a mistake. However good the men on the spot were at executive action, they needed continuous political guidance. Although there was great disappointment in some quarters at Maudling's fewer appearances on the scene, it pleased many in the Ulster Unionist Cabinet and according to the *Sunday Times*, which published a detailed report on the matter in the autumn of 1971, it pleased General Freeland also. They quoted him as saying that this freedom meant that 'there are not so many back seat drivers.' He was right, and more is the pity. The Joint Security Committee in Belfast, headed by the Northern Ireland Prime Minister, was now much freer to decide the tactics. In the days of the Labour Government the Committee was always guided by Whitehall, and questions about the use of the police, the separation of control, the routes of marches, would not have been left to be decided entirely by the Committee since I was likely to express some pretty forceful opinions on the political consequences of their actions. I reckoned, perhaps immodestly, that my political knowledge and instinct was of use in measuring the consequences of any proposed action by the Army and the Police. The *Sunday Times* referred to the change in the following manner: 'Under Labour scarcely a day had passed without, say, the Army Minister, Roy Hattersley, on the phone querying decisions as apparently trivial as the use of water-cannon.' The *Sunday Times* was right to say 'apparently trivial'. These matters are small in themselves, but they can have very large political consequences, and Hattersley was as aware as I was of the effect of some of the Army moves. Not everyone in the Army shared General Freeland's approval of his new-found liberty. General Farrar-Hockley, who was the Commander of the Land Forces under Freeland, is supposed to have said, 'When you're in unknown territory, it's useful to have native guides.' I agree, and regarded myself as one of the natives.

Making every allowance for the fact that Maudling was thrown in at the deep end, I have no doubt that the absence of political guidance between June 18 and July 5 led to much of the trouble during that period. Indeed those three weeks set the pattern almost irretrievably for the following three years' bloodshed. I shall never waver from my belief that the troubles of that summer might have been kept within compass if there had been firm political direction immediately after the change-over from the Labour to the Conservative Government.

Mr Maudling faced his first test within a few days of assuming office. When the Joint Security Committee met at Stormont on June 24, they were divided on whether to ban the following weekend's Protestant marches. It was a very troublesome decision to take, as we had found twelve months earlier. In the light of what had happened in 1969 I believe it would have been possible to have cancelled them. However, they decided not to do so. It was a defensible decision, but to allow the Protestants to march close to the Catholic areas was an indefensible blunder. The situation was already very sensitive in the Catholic areas because of the victory of the Conservative Party, with its long and continuous links with the Ulster Unionist Government. In the Protestant areas there was a sense of liberation. The Protestants felt that they were now in the ascendancy and were going to get an entirely new deal. I have been told on good authority that Mr Heath was informed of the likely consequences of allowing the march so near the Catholic areas. He was warned that it could lead to bloodshed. Had I been consulted I would certainly have backed such a view. There is no evidence that Maudling consulted anyone or that he took any steps to assess the position personally.

A further piece of ill luck for him was that Bernadette Devlin had been arrested after being refused leave to appeal to the House of Lords against the six-month sentence imposed on her for her part in the rioting in Londonderry the previous August. This combination of events coming just after the change of government made it easy for trouble-makers to convince the Catholic community that British

Government policy had changed. This was not so; what was true was that the Conservative Government was failing to give guidance to the men on the spot, and it was this which, in my judgement, led to the disastrous events of the next few days and opened the way for the Provisional IRA to pose, wrongly, as the only reliable defenders of the Catholic community.

The trouble began on the weekend of June 26-7 with stoning between rival mobs as the Protestants marched close to the Catholic areas. Suddenly gunfire broke out and five men, all Protestants, were shot dead. Nearly 250 others were injured, 58 of them by bullets. Police evidence is that a group of gunmen emerged from the mouth of Hooker Street in the Catholic Ardoyne area and fired at the Protestants. Their fire was then returned. There was more serious shooting at the Short Strand, a Catholic enclave in the middle of Protestant East Belfast, and here it seems likely that the Protestants began the shooting, which was replied to by the Catholic defenders. Later that night a number of British-owned departmental stores and industrial premises in Belfast were set on fire. Altogether it was estimated that £500,000 worth of damage had been done in the worst weekend's rioting that could be remembered, exceeding what had taken place in the summer of 1969. It was a terrible baptism for the Home Secretary, who had arranged to visit Belfast on Tuesday, June 30.

The visit passed off peacefully enough but Maudling seemed to be more of an observer than actively in charge of events. Even then criticism was increasing that the Army were not getting enough day-to-day guidance on the political implications of what they were doing and that generally it seemed as though the drive had gone out of the machine.

The events of the weekend after Maudling's visit confirmed those ill-wishers who wanted to believe that there had been a substantial change in government policy. I repeat that this was not so, but it was the lack of day-to-day or, where necessary, hour-to-hour guidance from the Government at Westminster which lent colour to this kind of accusation. What started it was that the Army had apparently received a tip-off about a substantial cache of arms. Correctly and sensibly, they immediately made a search and turned up pistols, rifles and a sub-machine-gun. Now there can be no complaint by any group, whether Catholic or Protestant, about the responsibility of the Army to uncover and remove arms caches of this sort, and no one can criticize them for doing so. What was different, however, is that during the lifetime of the Labour Government such a search would have been known beforehand to those who carried political responsibility and the extent and nature of it would have been agreed before the operation started, together with the response to be made if the troops suffered attack.

It happened on this particular occasion that as the last Army truck drew away after the search, it was stoned by a rapidly assembled mob of youths. It seems to me that on this occasion the Army over-reacted. They could not be expected to assess the political sensitivity of the area following the election of the new government in Britain, nor was it basically their responsibility to assess the consequences of carrying out an arms search immediately after the so-called triumphal marches of the Protestants the previous weekend and the open jubilation of extreme Unionists at Stormont and elsewhere. This was a job for the politicians. It is certainly arguable that a different decision should have been reached about the way in which the arms search was to be conducted, and whether other arms searches should take place in the Protestant areas at the same time.

That Friday evening the situation deteriorated rapidly and by 10 o'clock the Army declared a curfew over the whole of the Falls area. A tiny triangle of about 50 streets containing perhaps 5000 houses and covering a square mile, all within ten minutes walk of the centre of the capital city of Belfast, was completely sealed off. From a helicopter hovering in the darkness overhead the announce-ment was continuously broadcast over loud-hailers, 'This area is under curfew. You are to clear the streets immediately.' Officers on the ground announced through loud-hailers that people would not be allowed to go out to work, to shop or for any purpose whatsoever and that anyone on the streets after 10.30 p.m. would be arrested. They said that anyone seen firing a gun or carrying one would be shot. Two thousand troops combed slowly and meticulously through every house and street in the area and for 35 hours the whole of the Falls was sealed off. When the curfew was lifted five civilians were dead, dozens injured, and nearly 300 had been arrested, mostly for curfew-breaking and possessing explosives. The Army had a substantial haul of 20,000 rounds of ammunition and 107 assorted revolvers, rifles, automatic weapons and shotguns. Allegations of Army brutality and looting came thick and fast, and at the end of a few days a total of 334 complaints had been handed in at the special centres set up to receive them.

The adverse impact on the Catholic community was out of all proportion to the success of the Army's haul. The fact that the Army had operated purely on the Catholic side and had made no effort to go after Protestant arms caches led the Catholics to believe that the Army had changed sides. From now on they would be told that the Army was the servant of the Ulster Unionist Government and of the Protestants. This was the message of the Provisionals: only the Provisional IRA could safeguard the Catholic community. From now on they were on their own and had to look to themselves for their own defence. The Provisionals' seed-bed was well tilled and the harvest of tares was gathered in due time.

Once the weekend of July 3-5 was behind them, the Army had immediately to worry about the following weekend, when the massive Orange Order parades to celebrate the 280th Anniversary of the Battle of the Boyne were to take place. The leaders of the Order had brushed aside Maudling's plea to them to call off the marches as an 'act of humanity and magnanimity and to avoid possible bloodshed', so the security forces with a sinking heart and a high degree of apprehension settled down to the task of working out how to police the 100,000 or so Orangemen who were expected to take to the streets at 19 different centres all over the province. A large number of Catholics fled south in genuine fear to sit out the festivities in refugee camps over the border, and the Northern Ireland Government announced a 72-hour ban on the sale of alcohol.

All the evidence at this time points to a desire on the part of the government of the Republic to keep the temperature down. Mr Lynch and his colleagues had had a busy ten days before the marches took place. One of the most controversial of their actions was a visit by the then Foreign Minister, Dr Hillery, to the Falls Road area. He went unannounced, but the news of his visit was deliberately leaked afterwards and the Ulster Unionists were greatly incensed. What they probably did not realize at the time was that Hillery's visit was to pre-empt a much more inflammatory one that was to have been paid by Mr Neil Blaney, who was of course in violent opposition to Mr Lynch. Sir Alec Douglas-Home, I understand, had promised Mr Lynch maximum security for the Catholics during the Orange marching period and it was for this reason that Lynch took the exceptional steps that he did. He did not press for the July 12 march to be cancelled because he did not believe the situation would be improved if Chichester-Clark or the Orange Order were humiliated. Lynch also went on television and radio to make an eloquent plea for tolerance, reunification and Anglo-Irish friendship. He told the extremists on both sides of the border that there was no solution to be found to their disagreements by shooting each other. He appealed to the Catholics in the North and the South to ignore those few who would march in order to provoke them. To the Protestants he said: 'Do you mistrust yourselves so much as to refuse to see that your home is here – not across any waters? Since the Irish State was founded fifty years ago, my predecessors and I have said again and again that we have no wish to confront you or to destroy you. Do not be persuaded to sully your own great tradition.'

In the event, it turned out to be the strangest 'Twelfth' ever. The Orangemen marched in an orderly and sober manner under the watchful eye of 11,500 soldiers, 3500 policemen and 3700 members of the Ulster Defence Regiment. As one British Army intelligence officer commented afterwards: 'Security was so tight that a sparrow could not have coughed without getting arrested.' After the march was over, Stormont, acting on the principle of better late than never, decided to ban all further marches and processions for six months, the ban to include the Apprentice Boys' parade through Londonderry on August 12. Explaining the ban, Chichester-Clark said he was worried about the economic position and the rise in unemployment, pointing out, obviously enough, that 'industrialists are holding back, waiting to see what developments take place'.

The month of July did not end encouragingly, for watching industrialists or anyone else. The Army,who by now had added water-cannon and rubber bullets to their armoury, shot their first petrol bomber, and Belfast then suffered five nights of rioting on the trot, confirming a pattern which was soon to become the rule. The violence, which was exclusively Catholic, was aimed not at the Protestants but at the troops. Protestant cries for tougher action against the 'rebels' included ever louder demands for Chichester-Clark's resignation. Maudling hinted, as I had done months before, that direct rule might be a consequence of any swing to the right. The Northern Ireland Government meanwhile had announced a £50,000 reward for information leading to the conviction of anyone planting bombs, news which was greeted not long after with the province's one hundredth explosion of the year.

September ended in a flurry of change: Robert Porter, the moderate liberal barrister who had been all but overwhelmed at the Ministry of Home Affairs, resigned for reasons of health. More significantly, General Freeland and Sir Arthur Young, the twin heads of security, announced that they would be going too. Freeland was in the interesting and not unusual position of being at once hated by the Catholics for his toughness – a consequence of the Falls Road curfew – and reviled by the Protestants for being too 'soft'. Arthur Young, whom Porter had appointed in such a different atmosphere thirteen months earlier, was never so highly valued by Maudling, and without that support his work had been made increasingly difficult by Unionist demands for his replacement. I regretted the departure of the two top security chiefs within a short time of each other, and this, coupled with the new aggressive tactics of the Provisional IRA, and the political inactivity of the British Government, marked the beginning of a new and bloody phase. The final change was an apparent sinking of differences by some at least of the disparate elements that together formed Northern Ireland's parliamentary Opposition: five MPs and one Senator from almost as many different parties came together under Gerry Fitt's leadership as the Social Democratic and Labour Party with the 'eventual reunification of Ireland' as its main goal.

October, with the exception of a weekend riot in Londonderry, was relatively quiet – so quiet indeed that the Army, whose strength once again stood at 8000, let it be known that given another few weeks of peace it could begin to think about running down troop levels. But as the last weekend of the month was to show, the Army had counted its chickens too soon – or rather not counted its IRA men carefully enough. In two nights of carefully organized and controlled attacks, which included the emergence of the nail bomb as a terrorist weapon, 41 soldiers were injured, many severely. The Army rapidly announced that they were preparing to face a 'prolonged

IRA terrorist campaign'. The Provisional IRA's declaration of war was still to come, however, despite another 60 or so explosions in various parts of the province, many of them in traditional IRA style along the border. The year ended relatively quietly with a statement by the Northern Ireland Government that the troubles so far had cost an estimated £5½ million – in respect, that is, of such damage as is susceptible to costing.

1971 opened bleakly with a series of Catholic riots in Ballymurphy which brought in their train an apparently inevitable series of consequences. The right wing of the Unionist Party complained that the Army was too soft and demanded Chichester-Clark's resignation. Chichester-Clark then flew to London to demand an assurance, which Maudling duly gave, that the Army would get tough. Meanwhile, I was responding to a number of invitations that I had received after the general election from various groups to visit the Republic, and especially Dublin. As I had not been there for some years, I thought I would combine business with pleasure, and the Irish Ambassador in London, Donal O'Sullivan, was as helpful as always in arranging matters. He assured me that Mr Lynch's government would be happy to receive my wife and myself and eventually we paid a short visit from February 4-8, 1971. This was to be a fateful weekend in the history of Northern Ireland, although I did not realize it at the time.

On our arrival, we were picketed by Sinn Fein members, who circled quietly around the entrance to the airport, holding placards aloft calling for the withdrawal of British troops and shouting slogans. A strong group of Garda were there but their intervention was not called for. I began by having talks with Brendan Corish, the leader of the Irish Labour Party, who became Deputy Prime Minister in the Fine Gael/Labour Government after the March 1973 General Election. He is a charismatic personality who obviously has the right qualities to lead the Irish Labour Party. He was accompanied by Justin Keating, Minister for Industry in the Fine Gael/Labour Government, a very able man, and by the Secretary of the Party, Brendan Halligan. Unfortunately, Conor Cruise O'Brien, whom I admired very much, was away, but I knew his views on relations between North and South from our correspondence. He had always taken a more pessimistic view than I had of the prospects of building up a non-sectarian party in the North. He held the view, which I could not deny, that the politics of Northern Ireland had consistently been sectarian and tribal, because Northern Ireland itself had been created as a sectarian tribal society. Therefore, he said, Northern Ireland Protestants would always insist on preserving their majority status, while Northern Ireland Catholics fluctuated between revolting against their minority status and acquiescing in it. He believed that we socialists grossly underestimated the strength and durability of the sectarian tribal factors and that working-class unity between Protestants and Catholics in the North was as remote as it ever had been.

This made him very doubtful about the capacity of the Northern Ireland Labour Party to build itself up as a potent political force, because its potential development was restricted. On the other hand, Conor Cruise O'Brien always recognized that the Social Democratic and Labour Party could not hope to attract more than a marginal number of Protestant votes. So his solution was that the two parties should work closely together. I took the same view, but I believed that the British Labour Party should pin its official support to the Northern Ireland Labour Party because of its close links with the trade union movement which has always been a non-sectarian force in the North. The roots of the NILP go back to the formation of the first Independent Labour Party branch in the city of Belfast in 1893. It has survived ever since in one form or another, having been formally constituted as the Northern Ireland Labour Party in 1923. It has usually drawn rather more votes from Catholics than from Protestants, although it is totally non-sectarian in its composition. In the general election of 1970, it polled the useful total of 98,000 votes in seven constituencies, but it cannot be denied that its prospects are brightest when sectarian passions are lowest.

While in the Republic I had conversations with Liam Cosgrave, the leader of Fine Gael, who became Prime Minister after the March 1973 General Election. He was accompanied by Patrick Harte, the Member of Parliament for Donegal, Ritchie Ryan T.D., and Garrett Fitzgerald with whom I found a close sympathy. Fitzgerald later became Minister for Foreign Affairs, a task that he would obviously find congenial. Cosgrave's views of reunification and of future re-lations between North and South did not differ materially from those of Jack Lynch. Cosgrave is a quiet, sober man, but I formed the impression that he would have no mental hang-up in his relations with the IRA and might well deal with them more roughly that Lynch had. I also had conversations with the Confederation of Irish Industries about the prospects of co-operation with the North, and with the trades unions on the same subject. I naturally took the opportunity to visit the famous Abbey Theatre and then my wife and I spent a quiet weekend in Galway viewing some of the magnificent scenery of that part of the world. The Irish Government had been kind enough to arrange some separate events for my wife, who was particularly interested in visiting a children's hospital, especially since she is the Chairman of the Great Ormond Street Hospital for Sick Children.

One of the outstanding events of our visit was a long talk with Eamon De Valera. Naturally it was a great pleasure to meet this man who had helped to make so much of the history of modern Ireland and to hear him bring to life people who were only names to me and events which I had only read about. Indeed, the whole of our short visit was made more memorable by the many small gestures of kindness to my wife and myself by people we had never met before. For instance, when we stopped in Athlone for a cup of coffee and I walked down the street, the hotel proprietor insisted on coming out and presenting me with a gloriously knitted Irish sweater. I came home the richer by many tokens of friendship from these generous people.

Unfortunately the visit was marred by a new and grave turn of events in Belfast. This was the weekend on which the Provisionals declared war on the British Army. In some ways it was a response to the assurance that Maudling had given Chichester-Clark that the Army would get tough. On February 6, Gunner Robert Curtis, aged 20, was deliberately shot dead in an IRA machine-gun ambush. He was the first British soldier to die in action for over four years. The same night the Army shot dead two civilians, one of whom was a Provisional Staff Officer. The death of the British soldier and of the civilians caused a new shock wave to pass through Northern Ireland and its reverberation was felt in Dublin too. I spoke to Brendan Corish and sent messages to Mr Lynch and Mr Cosgrave, urging them if possible to unite in condemning this brutal attack on the British soldier and to demand that there should be no repetition of this violence. I was told that it was not possible for them to issue such a joint statement, but Mr Lynch put on record his deep regret and dismay at the tragic events which had taken place and unreservedly condemned those responsible, and the other two leaders took similar action.

My visit concluded with a long television interview. I said that I agreed wholly with Mr Lynch that you cannot permanently govern a people against their will if they feel deep grievances. The questioner was referring to the Catholics in the North, but I added that it would be equally true if the Protestants were to find themselves a minority in a United Ireland against their will. I emphasized, as Mr Lynch had done, that there was no grievance in Northern Ireland that was worth the loss of a single life. As regards the border, I admitted that it had now become an issue once again. In 1969, during the riots, I had uttered a remark that was to be often repeated: that the border was not an issue. At the time that I said it, it was true in relation to the immediate causes of the outbreaks of violence. They were caused by the demands for civil rights and the attacks by Protestants on Catholics. But of course the border is, and always has been, an underlying irritant at all times and as 1970 wore on it had come to the fore once again. I said that it would be a good thing if a unified Ireland could be achieved peacefully by the removal of the fears of the majority in the North. But it could not be achieved in any other way. As regards the IRA, I made it clear that although the Army could assist in warding off the intimidation which IRA leaders visited on some of the Catholic community, basically the people themselves must make up their minds that they would not live under a system of private justice administered by IRA personnel, with neither accountability nor responsibility. In the most constructive part of the interview I called for joint action by North and South to overcome some of the problems that are common to them both. I proposed that the two Governments should set up a new institution which I christened the All-Ireland Council to go to work on such matters as unemployment, the future of the West of Ireland and tourism.

The idea did not find favour at first, but I returned to it on a number of occasions, and Harold Wilson gave it much support.

Two years later in the spring of 1973, I felt very encouraged when the British Government announced they were in favour of such a body and were prepared to facilitate its formation.

There was no let-up in the IRA campaign. A few days after my visit a second British soldier was killed. The Army meanwhile had undergone two changes of command. Major-General Erskine Crum, who had succeeded General Freeland as GOC, suffered a heart attack only a fortnight after taking up his post. He was succeeded in his turn by General Sir Harry Tuzo.

Maudling gave no public indication of the serious turn of events. In an optimistic statement to the House of Commons in the middle of February, he announced that the reform programme had done much to reduce sectarian tensions. It was the very success of the reforms, he explained, that was provoking extremists to violence. This optimistic account did not recognize that the Provisionals had by this time seriously changed their tactics and were proceeding to wage an all-out war on the British Army.

Towards the end of the month, Lynch addressed the annual convention of the Fianna Fail Party in Dublin. 'Where it can be shown,' he said, 'that attitudes embodied in our law and constitution give offence to liberty of conscience, then we are prepared to see what can be done to harmonize our views so that a new kind of Irish society may be created equally agreeable to North and South.' Scarcely anyone, however, was in a mood to take up the olive branch, and by the time Maudling paid his second visit to Northern Ireland in March, the province was in a state of deep depression after suffering two of the most dismal months in its recent and turbulent history. Ten people were dead and dozens more had been injured in riots and gun battles. Addressing both houses of Stormont, an unprecedented occasion, Maudling said the present state of violence could not be tolerated but offered no clue how it might be brought to an end. As he was speaking troops opened fire during a riot in the Falls Road and a man was killed. Another soldier and a civilian died that night. Afterwards Gerry Fitt remarked sourly that Maudling's speech had contributed 'absolutely nothing'. John Hume said it would have been better if Maudling had stayed at home.

A week later there occurred the most shocking and horrible outrage of all up to this time; three off-duty Scottish soldiers of the Royal

Highland Fusiliers were murdered in cold blood in a country lane at Ligoniel three miles outside Belfast. Two of them were brothers, aged seventeen and eighteen. Their bodies were found lying in a heap under a hedge by children on their way to school. They had been shot in the head. Chichester-Clark, who feared that the long-heralded Protestant backlash was about to burst, flew to London on March 16, 1971, to demand what his brother, Robin, the Unionist MP at Westminster, was later to describe as 'specific and swift action' against the IRA.

Chichester-Clark's main demands have not been published, but I understood at the time that his Cabinet had called for a large increase in the number of troops in Northern Ireland, in addition to extended curfews, though only in the Catholic sectors, and searches of streets by blocks, going from house to house. To have conceded such demands would have been to admit that as the Government could not isolate the IRA, they were determined to punish the Catholic community as a whole. This was almost certainly in the Stormont Government's mind, but it was not Maudling's way of doing things, nor that of Lord Carrington, the Defence Secretary. The British Government, at that stage, was still hoping for a political solution and still believed that the reforms would be enough in themselves. Unfortunately, although they wanted a political solution, they did not will the means and at no stage took the initiatives that were necessary to achieve it. Accordingly they met only one of Chichester-Clark's demands, namely for more troops, and he returned to Belfast with a promise of 1300 extra – he had asked for 3000 – and even so the effect was partly offset because Tuzo let it be known that he did not want any more anyway. Chichester-Clark himself was sensible enough to know that more troops was not the way to counter a campaign of IRA terrorists, but he needed them basically for a political reason, namely to try to roll back the adverse tide of opinion within his own party. He failed. Four days later he resigned, to be succeeded by Brian Faulkner, who at last gained the office he had waited for, by defeating William Craig, his only opponent, by 26 votes to 4.

The resignation of Chichester-Clark and the appointment of Faulkner as Prime Minister coincided with a visit to Northern Ireland that I had arranged some time previously. It was an official visit on behalf of the British Labour Party, and the other members of the delegation were Sir Harry Nicholas, the General Secretary, and Mr Ron Hayward, the National Organizer, who later succeeded Harry Nicholas. The purpose of our visit was to try to build support for the Northern Ireland Labour Party. I had long cherished the idea of building up the NILP, and a month after we left office on July 22, 1970, I wrote to Harry Nicholas saying: 'The path to peace in Northern Ireland and to good relations with the government of the Republic lies in bringing together in one party both the Protestant and Catholic working-class men and women, as well as the professional classes and others from among those who have been the guiding spirits in the recent political upsurge. The Northern Ireland Labour Party's platform must be based on the economic and social needs of the electorate. It follows that our policy would not be successful if we seemed to be appealing for support to only one section of the community, namely the Catholics, although it is probably true to say that in the last General Election the majority of our votes came from Catholics together with what I might call a Protestant conscience vote.'

I went on: 'The party must continue to accept that partition cannot be ended except by consent, but we should work for the creation of conditions in which the people of Ireland feel sufficient confidence in each other to enable constitutional developments to take place between North and South. In appealing, as we should do, to people on both sides of the religious frontiers, we shall be attacking the very foundation of the Ulster Unionist power which has been frankly based on an appeal to Protestants as opposed to Catholics. As an organization, it is clear that the Northern Ireland Labour Party does not have the financial resources nor the numbers to enable it to present itself as an alternative government to the Ulster Unionists. Other groups like the New Ulster Movement are too middle class in origin and appear to be at the centre of the political scene.

My hope was that we could set up constituency parties with a powerful Northern Ireland Council of Labour actively backed by the trade unions, with the object in due course of contesting all the seats for Stormont and several for the Westminster elections. I recognized that it would need a lot of organization and a substantial period of time in order to get the set-up right. I concluded by saying:

'This may be over-ambitious and may fail as other attempts have done in the past, but I am firmly convinced that we should make the effort. If we are to succeed it will be necessary to break the domination of the Ulster Unionist Party. This may be historically the moment to do it for their grip is feebler than it has been at any time since 1921.'

I was right in my analysis of the feebleness of the Ulster Unionist Party but also over-optimistic in my hopes for trying to establish non-sectarian politics. Nevertheless, although our attempt failed it will have to be made again, for there can be no real future for Northern Ireland until strong non-sectarian parties have been built. The National Executive Committee had agreed that we should make the effort and accordingly Harry Nicholas, Ron Hayward and I set off for Northern Ireland on the very weekend that Chichester-Clark was replaced by Faulkner.

On our arrival at Belfast I was at once asked by pressmen about Mr Faulkner and I said I hoped he would succeed in his efforts. He had been a full party to the reforms that had been introduced and had shown a lot of courage in pushing through the local housing reforms. I wished him success.

In our arrangements we were fortunate that Harry Nicholas had close links with Senator Kennedy of the Transport and General Workers' Union and he smoothed our path throughout the whole of our visit. We were accompanied by Vivian Simpson, the only Northern Ireland Labour Party Member of Parliament at Stormont, and Erskine Holmes, the Chairman of the Party, among a number of others. They had arranged a large rally in the Ulster Hall in Belfast, together with visits to Lisburn, Lurgan, Portadown, Armagh, Newry and Dungannon. It was a very punishing schedule.

In our effort to introduce non-sectarian politics in Ireland, we soon found ourselves caught in a full sectarian crossfire. When I visited the Mayor and other civic authorities at Lisburn, I was met by a group of women on the pavement outside the Town Hall shouting; 'No Surrender and No Pope. And Go Home Lundy (addressed to me).' There was also another Protestant demonstration at Portadown, where I was jeered by Protestants carrying the Union Jack who were under the mistaken impression because the Mayor was present at lunch that the cost was being borne by the rates, and had a placard complaining about it. That was not the only example of muddled thinking, for they told me in pretty brusque terms that I had no right to come to Portadown while in the next breath insisting that they were an integral part of the United Kingdom. I found this logic a little difficult to understand, but they could see no inconsistency when I pointed it out. We had good meetings in all these towns, usually with an invited audience. At Dungannon I was angered to be told that some people were standing outside the restaurant in which the meeting took place, writing down the names of everybody who attended. They were not doing so with any friendly intent. At Newry I was greeted, jostled and hustled by a group of Sinn Fein members and IRA supporters who followed me down the street and back again and clamoured loudly when they were excluded from the hall in which I was meeting those called together by the Newry Labour Party. It was quite a stormy scene outside, and when the Republican sympathizers found they would not be admitted, since it was obviously their intention to break up the meeting if they were allowed in, they stood outside the windows singing loudly and in disharmony 'Go Home You Bum', continuously, for about 20 minutes.

However, at all these places we had very useful and helpful meetings and there was a striking contrast between the extremists who jostled and jeered on both sides, and the sensible, sober, well-meaning but troubled people who met me inside the halls. I had another example of this in the Butler Street Community Hall in the Ardoyne. This was notorious as a no-go area. Right-wing Unionists claimed that the Ardoyne was ruled by terrorists and IRA gunmen and was barred to the police. The truth was somewhat more complicated. As far as I could ascertain, the Ardoyne was patrolled day and night by troops on foot and in mobile units at the time that I was there, and no one questioned it. By day, too, the RUC worked openly in the area making inquiries and delivering summonses. But after nightfall police officers were reluctant to patrol the darkened streets and back alleys on foot, and in the months before my visit, the districts had been the scene of a murderous feud between the two wings of the IRA in which at least five men had been shot and others had been tortured in back rooms. Apart from this horrible development, the Ardoyne was used to not being well policed. In many ways it reminded me of some areas in London and certain of our own seaports about fifty years ago, where police were equally reluctant to go after nightfall and sometimes during the day. These were tough areas and the Ardoyne was somewhat similar.

I walked through Butler Street to the Community Hall in daylight and surrounded by a friendly group of people. Inside the hall was an even larger crowd of men and women and children, but I could not help noticing as I talked to them that Republican and IRA sympathizers had pushed in too. Whereas I got a generally friendly reception, these were the hostile people who put an edge on their questions and were openly aggressive. Their message was: 'Take the British troops out of Northern Ireland and abolish the Special Powers Act.' I argued the question out with them, as I had done on previous occasions, and at one point I said very heatedly in response to frequent challenges from an IRA sympathizer: 'If you'd stop shooting at British soldiers there would be no need to use the Special Powers Act.' There was widespread agreement among the great majority of people in the hall when I said this, but it was also clear to me that these determined and fanatical young men could and would take control of the situation, despite the lack of sympathy among many of those in their community. It was easy enough for me to stand up to them for I was not part of the neighbourhood, but it would have taken a lot of courage for anybody to oppose them who lived and worked in the area in which they operated.

The Social Democratic and Labour Party leaders were not anxious to meet me and I was not surprised, for I was there to build up the Northern Ireland Labour Party. Gerry Fitt said, naturally, that he regarded our visit as inopportune and divisive. He himself showed a lot of courage in standing up to the Provisional IRA, as did John Hume and other members of the SDLP. There was always an undertone of sympathy among a number of the members of the Parliamentary Labour Party for Gerry Fitt, but it seemed to me that the SDLP had a basic weakness in that it could only appeal to one community. It was our endeavour to appeal across the frontiers to two communities, Protestant and Catholic alike, in order to try to get a firm basis for non-sectarian politics. In doing this we intended to rely very much on the trade unions for support and I was well aware from my previous contacts that the trade union leaders, and even more, their members, would be unlikely to support the SDLP, whereas there was a substantial hope that they could be brought to support the Northern Ireland Labour Party. Trade unions are not in a strong position politically in Northern Ireland, for the system of contracting in applies to the political levy, that is to say a member of a trade union has positively to opt to pay the political levy, whereas in the rest of the United Kingdom he pays it automatically as part of his subscription unless he positively contracts out of the payment.

My first meeting was with a number of shop stewards and this was followed by other meetings with church leaders, university lecturers, workers in Harland and Wolff, farmers, and civic leaders in most of the major towns.

The Ulster Hall was crowded for a great meeting and nearly 1500 people were present. My message was the same there as everywhere else that I went. There was an urgent need to build up the NILP on non-sectarian lines so that it could take the place of the Ulster Unionist Party which was crumbling. Stormont should be larger and therefore more representative, more Members of Stormont were needed, elected possibly on the basis of proportional representation. Britain stood firm on the constitutional position on the border – that is to say, that it could only be changed by consent – but there was a strong case for much more cooperation both politically and economically between the North and the South.

I suggested a number of matters for their consideration – a Corporation to bring in public industries, a development bank that could supply capital at preferential rates, schemes for better marketing of agricultural produce, and co-operation in the purchase of fertilizers, etc. Basically I said it was for them – not others – to work out their own social and economic programme to overcome the horrifying unemployment levels and improve the dreary housing conditions. The British Labour Party would undertake to give the NILP all help in such a programme.

The response of the meeting was enthusiastic and was made even better by the presence of a small number of virulent Protestant women extremists in the gallery who inadvertently helped me a great deal by their interruptions. The incoming Prime Minister, Brian Faulkner, had invited our Delegation to lunch and in the course of it he told me that during the morning he had asked David Bleakley, former Chairman of the Northern Ireland Labour Party and a well-known and respected member of the Party, to become the Minister for Community Relations. I was glad to hear this, as it showed signs of a new approach by Faulkner. Bleakley is a well-known pioneer of community relations in his own area, well respected throughout Northern Ireland, and a man of deep principle and religious convictions.

He had begun the day as usual, teaching at the Methodist College, Belfast, when he was summoned to Stormont and offered the Cabinet post. I asked him privately at lunch whether he would accept and he told me that he had decided to do so. Bleakley made up his mind to accept without any consultation with me, and I put this on record only because it was alleged that I had persuaded him to take the post. I would have been ready to do so but it was not necessary. He agreed to become a Minister for six months and endeavour to see whether he could do some useful work. At the end of that time he resigned, his task having been made impossible by internment and civil disobedience. Looking back, I have no doubt that he was right to make the effort. Naturally his acceptance caused some division in the Northern Ireland Labour Party, but the overwhelming majority of the Party supported the decision he had taken, even though there was an ironical Irish flavour about it for we were busy attacking the Ulster Unionists at that very moment. The reporting of the visit by the Press was generally friendly and the London *Times* was good enough to say that it could be counted a major success in personal and political terms. But on the return home I felt despondent, having once again experienced at first hand the depths of sectarianism. It seemed to me that the gallant and principled members of the Northern Ireland Labour Party were doomed to fight a lone and losing battle for the time being. But I hope they will continue their efforts and never lose heart. They are a gallant group of men and women whose principles hold the key to the future of Northern Ireland and I pay tribute to their courage.

12

In the first three months that Faulkner was Prime Minister, there were more than 160 major explosions in the province: the bomb had become the Provisionals' chief weapon of attack. None the less, on June 22, the 50th anniversary of the opening of Stormont by King George V and Queen Mary, Faulkner, pursuant to his undertakings when Bleakley accepted office, offered the Opposition significantly greater participation in major policy-making. He proposed a system of three committees, two of which would be chaired by Opposition MPs, to consider new policy in the fields of social services, industry and environment. At first the Opposition showed interest, then they began to have doubts, and finally the whole idea was overtaken by the relentless grind of events.

Early in July, after four nights of rioting in the Bogside, troops shot two young Catholics dead, Seamus Cusack and Desmond Beattie. Local people claimed that neither was armed and that at least one of them was no Republican. The SDLP issued the British Government with a hasty ultimatum: unless they set up an immediate and independent public inquiry into the deaths of the two men, the SDLP would withdraw from Stormont. The inquiry was refused and the six MPs accordingly withdrew, announcing that they would establish an alternative Parliament. Meanwhile the slide into disaster was accelerating. As July 12 came round again, the ninth British soldier was killed. The tenth died the following day and on July 17 the Provisionals blew up the *Daily Mirror*'s new printing plant just outside Belfast. Built at a cost of £2 million, it never reopened. Towards the end of the month, the Army instituted a series of dawn raids on the homes of suspected IRA members and sympathizers in an attempt to find membership and other records, and in response 11 huge explosions rocked the province in one night.

With the peace now constantly disturbed both by day and night, people's nerves were becoming ever tauter. And it was inevitable that the word 'internment' should start to appear in discussion of what should be done. My belief is that Faulkner became reconciled to the need for internment as the summer wore on and explosions increased only because he could think of no other method of dealing with the IRA. The restive Protestant majority, which had ousted Chichester-Clark, was now becoming increasingly critical of him. Certainly, the people of Northern Ireland had much to put up with, and I could fully understand their feeling of exasperation and that something should be done.

It is always a difficult moment for governments, when solutions are unclear but public opinion demands immediate action. It is then that Ministers tend to make their worst mistakes, and it happened once again on this occasion. It is said that Chichester-Clark used to stall demands for internment by seeking military and police advice on the subject. This used to get him off the hook for they always gave the same answer – No. The security forces were in my experience opposed to internment as a means of settling the problem or of improving the situation. In their view, internment would make matters worse. But Faulkner was driven to consider it because he could think of no other way of dealing with the violence. And on this side of the Channel, the British Cabinet had exhausted whatever arsenal of counter-proposals they had, which was small enough. For neither Faulkner nor the British Government were ready to consider the kind of political proposals that would have improved the prospects of Catholic co-operation, because of their fear of adverse Protestant reaction.

So the situation drifted from bad to worse. Internment eventually became the panacea because it was the only untried instrument the Protestants could think of. Right up to the end, there is no evidence that the Army, or General Tuzo, or the majority of the RUC favoured internment as a policy. It is very doubtful that either Maudling or Carrington did. But they were all caught in the same trap. Something had to be done to halt the explosions and no one could think of any other solution. Of course alternative solutions were there and could have been tried, and I did my best to put them forward in the House of Commons, for internment on a large scale and unaccompanied by political measures was always doomed to

be a dead end. It was obvious to anyone who thought about
the matter that it could not be successful unless Lynch co-operated
in the South and helped to seal the escape routes. But so far as
I know, no private governmental approach was made to him.
Instead he was subjected to a long range bombardment of public
speeches. The information about the Provisionals and the IRA
was patchy, although it was better in respect of the long-established
Official IRA.

The Labour Party had been pressing for a debate on the deteriora-
ting situation for some weeks during the summer, but pressure on the
Parliamentary timetable arising from such matters as the ill-fated
Industrial Relations Act had made it impossible to hold one.
Eventually, we were able to secure a debate on the very day that
Parliament was due to rise. By coincidence it was the day on which
Faulkner was in London to attend the Cabinet to press for internment, although we were not to know that at that time. Normally
on the day of an Adjournment, the House is nearly empty except
for a handful of Members who wish to speak on their own particular
subjects. On this morning when I rose at 11 a.m. to speak, the sun-
light was shafting through the Chamber and fell on well occupied
benches. Not only my own speech but that of nearly everyone else
expressed the deep foreboding that we all felt.

On the question of internment I had naturally thought much
in the days that preceded the debate and had consulted the
Shadow Cabinet about it. As I expected, I found them strongly
opposed, but concerned, as everyone was, that events seemed to be
moving inexorably towards it in the absence of any alternative
policies. It was my task in the debate, therefore, to try to put forward
an alternative that might stand a chance. Although I was not to
know it at the time, I had to make my speech even while the Cabinet
was assembling to decide the issue. They were not present to hear me.

I began by expressing the deep sense of foreboding I felt about
the situation. I did not think I had ever approached a debate on
Ireland with a deeper sense of impending tragedy than I did on that
day. I spoke of the changed role of the Army since 1969. Then it had
gone to Northern Ireland in order to keep the peace between the
communities, but now, especially because of the declaration of war
by the Provisional IRA, the Army was finding itself increasingly

engaged in hunting down individual IRA members. I thought it right also to put on record that in spite of the complaints that I constantly received about actions by individual soldiers, it was my deep belief that no other Army faced with such provocation and faced also with the burden of handling a political problem that Westminster and Stormont had failed to solve, would have conducted itself with the restraint that the British Army had shown.

I then referred to Maudling, saying that I recognized that he was surrounded by a multitude of counsellors offering different advice. But whatever advice he was getting, it was important that he should do more to give the appearance of activity. While I recognized his massive common sense, I wished that on occasions he would use less common sense and more psychology. I then turned to the main part of my speech whose theme was basically the need for a double-headed approach in which additional security precautions should go hand in hand with new political initiatives. There was an absolute need to bring the Republic of Ireland more into events, both on the security side and in relation to the political situation. My first proposal, therefore, was that Mr Lynch should be invited to come to this country immediately, a proposition that found considerable support on the Labour benches, and that while here he should meet both the Prime Minister, Mr Heath, and Mr Faulkner. On the security side, I proposed that there should be common action, particularly in relation to the patrolling of the border and to the taking of legal and other action against the IRA. I used the words 'other action' because I recognized that there might be a need for action against the IRA by both governments that would not be subject to the full legal process. I pointed out that the IRA were no more supporters of Mr Lynch than they were of Mr Faulkner: they would wreck Ireland if they could get control.

I went on to say that action should also be taken against those Protestants who held guns, and that these should be handed over to the authorities. If that was not done, then action should be taken in other ways and by the authorities.

Politically, I proposed that the Prime Minister and Mr Faulkner should discuss with Mr Lynch the suggestion that I had put forward in Dublin some months earlier for a council of All Ireland. I recognized that at that stage it would have no legislative or administrative responsibility. But I proposed that there should be a meeting of members of both Stormont and the Dail in order to discuss problems of mutual concern to both North and South, and especially such matters as unemployment, regional development, industrial development and other matters. It was necessary increasingly for North and South to work together if the IRA was to cease to be a threat to both countries, because their activities could undoubtedly spread from the North to the South.

I concluded by emphasizing once again that additional security measures and new political initiatives must come together and at the same time. They could not be separated, and I begged the Home Secretary not to take any one of my proposals out of its context. I believed that if there was to be any chance of pulling ourselves out of the situation into which Northern Ireland had drifted, then there must be a new package and that it was necessary for all the items to go together.

My speech was not long – it took a little over twenty minutes – but Mr Maudling's was even shorter. He had hardly got to his feet before he sat down again. He spoke only for four minutes. He praised what I had said, and thanked me for the constructive way in which I phrased my speech. He promised me careful study of my suggestions. Then he went to the Cabinet meeting and they ignored every word of what I had said. My general proposal for an All-Ireland Council was supported by Kevin McNamara of Hull North, and by Gerry Fitt. But Conservative speakers like Angus Maude and Captain Willie Orr, while agreeing with me about the seriousness of the situation, offered no encouragement for my political proposals, or for the All-Ireland-Council. They were concerned basically with putting right the security situation. Even while we were speaking, Mr Faulkner was persuading the British Cabinet that internment, coupled with the cancellation of the Orange marches, was the proper policy. I wish that Maudling and Carrington and others who knew of the situation had fought harder against Faulkner on this occasion.

It is my belief that events in the following months might have been different and many lives might have been saved if proposals similar to those I had put forward in the debate had been followed. I fully recognize the feelings of the Protestant majority in Northern

Ireland. But while they had a lot to put up with before internment, let us look in cold figures at what happened subsequently. In the 24 months prior to internment, 66 people had been killed, including 11 soldiers. In the first 17 months after internment, 610 were killed, of whom 146 were soldiers. Was it necessary to wade through this river of blood in order to achieve an understanding with Mr Lynch about a joint attitude towards the IRA and to secure the next political steps? I cannot believe it was.

After internment had been brought in, it was freely said that I had been consulted about it and had agreed. This is not so. The first I knew of the decision was when Faulkner and Maudling both telephoned me separately early in the morning of August 9 to tell me that the operation had taken place. If I had been told or consulted, I would have repeated what I said in the House of Commons, that it would be wrong and counter-productive to take action on the security question without also taking political action at the same time.

When the Cabinet broke up on August 5, the only public announcement was that another 1800 troops would be sent to Ulster. The weekend that followed saw vicious IRA and Catholic rioting in Belfast, and at dawn on August 9 the Army swooped to put in force the Cabinet's decision. By that evening nearly 350 people had been arrested. However, the Provisionals had not been taken by surprise. The move was rumoured for days; Belfast newspapers had been full of advertisements for prison officers. When the Army banged on their doors at 4 a.m. most of the leading Provisionals were elsewhere. Four days later they held a press conference in Belfast to prove it. Their leader, Joe Cahill, described the arrests as a pinprick.

It is doubtful whether anyone, including myself, foresaw just how violent the Catholic reaction to internment would be. Certainly they could not have foreseen how ineffectual it would prove as an answer to terrorism. Thirty-six hours after the swoop, 15 people had died, one of them a Catholic priest, Father Hugh Mullen, shot while administering the last rites. It was more than had died in such a brief period at any time since the 1920s. In Belfast 300 houses had been burnt out, another black record for the city. As for the rest, it was much as it had been in August two years before: barricades were thrown up round the Catholic areas, vehicles of every description were hi-jacked, petrol bombs and CS gas were exchanged through nights of ferocious rioting, and Belfast echoed to the rattle of small arms and machine-gun fire. Also, once again, hundreds of families from mixed areas of Catholics and Protestants were on the move. Six weeks later it was estimated that 8000 people had shifted from one part of the city to another in a desperate retreat into the safety of their respective ghettoes. Forty-eight hours after the raids the death toll had risen to 23; 230 of those arrested had been served with detention orders. Mr Heath, meanwhile, had gone sailing on *Morning Cloud*.

Faulkner took the opportunity to issue a White Paper called a 'Record of Constructive Change' which detailed the reforms that had been put in hand. He denied that the implementation of them had been delayed, claiming that since June 1969 no less than 12 of them had become law, despite the civil unrest during that time. The only legislation outstanding related to the complex matter of local government reorganization. One man, one vote, was now law; two Ombudsmen had been appointed, one to deal with allegations of Government maladministration, the other with complaints against local councils and public bodies; a Ministry of Community Relations and a Community Relations Commission had both been in existence for nearly two years; the new housing executive was taking over responsibility for all publicly owned housing, which was allocated now according to an impartial points system; all statutory bodies and almost all local authorities had made a declaration of equality of employment opportunity; the B-Specials had been disbanded and the RUC, which had been disarmed, was controlled by a separate police authority; an Act to impose penalties for incitement to hatred and the circulation of false statements was in force; and the task of prosecuting offenders would shortly be taken out of the hands of the police and given to a Director of Public Prosecutions modelled on the English system. It is a good record.

Faulkner had been provoked by a speech in which Lynch had called for the replacement of the Stormont Government by an administration in which power and decision-making would be equally shared by Unionists and non-Unionists. Stormont, Lynch said, had always dedicated itself to suppressing the civil and human rights of the Catholic minority and was therefore responsible for the recurring violence in the North. Faulkner in reply accused Lynch of cant and hypocrisy, adding that the IRA now engaged in a murderous battle with British troops, trained, organized and enjoyed a safe haven in the South. He went on to assure the Catholics in the North that Lynch's 'blatant attempt to use them as political pawns' would not sway him from his determination to ensure a full part in Northern Ireland's affairs for those 'who are prepared to accept their responsibilities as well as assert their rights'. It was the act of internment which had reduced the two Prime Ministers to such exchanges, and in this, as in so much else, internment produced more evil than the ills it sought to overcome.

At the end of August, the Northern Ireland Labour Party announced their proposals for a 'community government'. This was to be a two-year period of social reconstruction during which Faulkner would lead a coalition administration in which both Catholics and Protestants would be represented and after which new elections would be held according to a system of proportional representation. Their object was to isolate the terrorists on both sides, offer Catholic representatives a fair share in government, and strengthen the basis of Stormont. Faulkner dismissed the plan as unrealistic, although he did add that he welcomed some aspects of it. Announcement of the proposals was followed by a meeting in London between the British Labour Party, the Northern and Southern Irish Labour Parties, and the SDLP. It was a sort of socialist summit whose aim was to produce a solution to the crisis which would have the backing of socialists on both sides of the border. It was the first time we had all come together, although even so the Northern Ireland Labour Party and the SDLP agreed to meet only over lunch. We decided to set up a joint commission of inquiry into Northern Ireland, an idea which was later overtaken by Maudling's proposed round-table talks.

Meanwhile the death toll since internment had risen to 30 and the 300th bomb of the year had exploded with virtually no warning and devastating effect at the Belfast Headquarters of the Northern Ireland Electricity Board. One person died and 35 people were injured, 14 of them very seriously. One woman had to have 90 stitches in her face and head. A week later three bombs exploded without warning and almost simultaneously in the centre of Belfast at lunchtime. That evening a little Catholic girl aged 17 months was shot dead as she played in the street with her sister. She had been hit by an IRA bullet meant for a passing Army patrol. The wave of revulsion against the terrorists was so strong after these incidents that three days later the Provisional IRA were driven to announcing what they called a five-point peace plan. They offered a cease fire from midnight on September 9 if the Government would agree to end the troops' 'campaign of violence', abolish Stormont, establish a regional Parliament for a nine-county Ulster as a first step towards a united Ireland, release all political prisoners, and pay compensation to all those who had suffered, Nobody paid very much attention to their ultimatum and the day after it expired the 20th British soldier was shot dead.

The terrorists' latest atrocities had two other consequences. An opinion poll published by the *Daily Mail* at this time found that 59 per cent of those questioned in Britain were in favour of bringing the troops home from Northern Ireland – thereby meeting the first of the Provisionals' demands – and only 35 per cent were against the idea. Secondly, 20,000 Protestants gathered at a rally in Belfast to express their frustration and anger at the anarchy sweeping through the province. The speakers, who included Paisley, said the time had come to form what they called a third force, in other words an irregular militia of armed Protestants. This was soon to emerge, first in the form of locally based vigilante groups and later under the umbrella of the Ulster Defence Association.

Political initiatives now were much in the air. Heath and Lynch, after a singularly acrimonious and public exchange of telegrams over internment, met at Chequers to try and patch things up, while Maudling announced his plans for round-table talks. The SDLP promptly denounced these as totally unacceptable. They said they would talk to no one until internment had been ended and all the detainees released, a position to which they were to cling steadfastly during the next year, bedevilling attempts to get all the sides talking.

Towards the end of September Parliament was recalled at our request for a two-day debate on Northern Ireland. During the debate I said that one of the Conservative Government's mistakes had been to regard the 1969 reform programme as if it was something enshrined in the tablets and left nothing more to do. The Home Secretary, I said, should have pursued the residual problems with greater energy. The Government had stood back and allowed Faulkner to make the running, the result of which had been to drive the minority into a more extreme position. Internment, I repeated, if undertaken should have been accompanied by a real political initiative. Terrorists who shot at British soldiers had no right to be at liberty but the evidence was that those interned at present covered a far wider spectrum than that, and I called for a commission to investigate the evidence against each internee.

October 1971 saw no let-up in the level of violence. It was said at the time that there was scarcely a working-class person in Northern Ireland who did not know someone who had been killed or injured. When Stormont reassembled after the summer recess, the Opposition had been reduced to the solitary presence of Vivian Simpson, of the Northern Ireland Labour Party. Later in the month the alternative Parliament set up by the SDLP and calling itself the Assembly of the Northern Irish People, met for the first time under the presidency of John Hume in a ballroom in Dungiven. It had a certain curiosity value but not much more. Faulkner published a Green Paper: 'The Future Development of the Parliament and Government of Northern Ireland', containing proposals for proportional representation and an enlarged Commons and Senate. But they were only proposals, not commitments, and attracted very little attention. It was too little, too late.

There was no restraint on the streets. At the end of September two public houses in the Belfast Protestant heartlands of Sandy Row and the Shankill had been wrecked by terrorist bombs. Two people died and more than 50 were injured. The Protestants naturally took this for the slap in the face it was meant to be, and the activities of their vigilante groups increased enormously as a result. Soon thousands of men working in four-hour shifts were vigorously enforcing a system of road blocks and barricades around every Protestant working-class district in the city. Under this sort of pressure Faulkner called for yet tougher security measures and suggested that the vigilantes should be organized on the 'official' basis. He reassured his supporters that internment had led to the capture of 63 officers and 96 volunteers of the Provisional IRA and 33 officers and 28 volunteers of the Official IRA. In September alone, he said, a further 266 people had been arrested under the Special Powers Act. He then flew to London for talks with Heath, returning, as usual, with yet more troops – bringing the total in Ulster to a record 14,000 – and a promise that minor roads across the border with the South would be blown up – another gesture. The objective for Faulkner was to try to calm Protestant fears and threats, and for Heath to counter recurring charges of inactivity and inertia. By January 1972, most of the 160-odd 'unapproved' crossing points had been blocked by concrete posts erected by the Army, leaving some 50 others along a border 300 miles long.

Two other developments were causing some concern to the authorities. Immediately after internment the Catholics had instituted a rent and rates strike by way of an effective and, it must be said, personally painless protest. Two months later Stormont estimated that up to 140,000 people living in local authority housing were taking part, and the loss in revenue was put at £400,000. The need for cash, too, was behind a staggering series of armed hold-ups of post offices and banks on both sides of the border. After the twenty-fifth armed robbery in three months Desmond O'Malley, the Irish Minister of Justice, told his Cabinet that armed criminals were moving freely about the country and holding it to ransom. At the same time, Stormont reckoned that nearly £100,000 had been stolen in 48 raids since the beginning of the year. No one doubted that it was the work of the IRA pay corps. Meanwhile the campaign of violence intensified. Twenty-seven people died during October and 148 were injured. There were 140 major explosions. Ruari O'Bradaigh, the Provisionals' President, explained in a newspaper interview that the bombing was designed to damage the Northern economy as part of an overall campaign to bring about British withdrawal. The first half of the proposition at any rate had a considerable propaganda success, especially when Roy Bradford, the Stormont Minister of Development, announced a few days later that the province was 'facing bankruptcy'. Five people, including two women, were shot dead during the last bloody weekend of October, during which the Provisionals held their annual conference in Dublin and promised an 'accelerated programme of violence'. They were apparently true to their word: the following week three soldiers were killed and ten policemen's homes were bombed in one night. Six RUC men died within three weeks.

Most political debate at this time centred on the much disputed question of internment. The *Sunday Times* gave it considerable impetus with their revelations about the methods of interrogation used on IRA suspects at the Palace Barracks just outside Belfast. They published a series of sworn statements by detainees who alleged that they had been deprived of food and sleep for prolonged periods and kept standing for hours against a wall in cruelly uncomfortable positions with hoods over their heads and subjected all the while to a continuous high-pitched throbbing noise. A Commission of Inquiry set up under the Chairmanship of Sir Edmund Compton to investigate these and other allegations duly reported that although some detainees had been ill-treated – the original allegations were not denied – none had been subjected to physical brutality or cruelty. Later another commission was set up under Lord Parker, the former Lord Chief Justice, to inquire into methods of interrogation. By a majority of two to one, Lord Gardiner nobly dissenting, the Committee leant over backwards to try to justify most of the techniques. Heath, however, very wisely spurned their efforts and announced that such methods would not be used again.

During the first 90 days after internment, that is between August 9 and November 6, 1971, a total of 882 people were arrested under the Special Powers Act. At the end of the period 476 had been released, 278 had been interned, 112 detained and 16 were being held for interrogation.

I had been attacked at the Labour Party Conference in October for refusing to condemn the policy of internment out of hand. What I said there was that internment was a loathsome weapon sanctioned by no peaceful or just society. I said that two Labour MPs, Merlyn Rees and Kevin McNamara, on a recent visit to an internment camp had been confronted by a body of 50 to 60 internees, who drew themselves up in three ranks in military formation and behaved as though they were prisoners of war, refusing to speak until their officers told them to. How do you get out of that situation, I asked. Do you release them? I went on to say that, in my judgement, many were interned who ought not to be and repeated my proposal that an independent judicial tribunal, perhaps under a Commonwealth judge, should examine the evidence against each internee. We were talking of the stark reality of force, I reminded the delegates, and we had to reconcile the principles we all held with ensuring that people could go about their lives without fear of violence. I added, once again, that internment on the scale on which it had been introduced and enforced, without any political initiatives, had polarized the communities and if its intention had been to ensure peace it had singularly failed. The Conference accepted my statement.

During the autumn, the British Labour Party took the initiative in holding two further conferences with the Northern Ireland Labour Party, the Social Democratic and Labour Party and the Irish Labour Party. These occasions were not very easy because of the difficulty of trying to establish a common view. Our hope was that all the parties could agree to proposals for presentation to the Government of Northern Ireland and to the Government at Westminster, as well as to the Government of the Republic. But this did not prove possible. At this time both Harold Wilson and I were very much in favour of trying to secure inter-party talks at Westminster between the Government and ourselves, to be followed by talks with the Northern Ireland Labour Party, the Social Democratic and Labour Party and the Unionist Party, and at a slightly later stage with Mr Lynch. While the Government at times seemed in favour of the idea, they blew hot and cold and it never really got off the ground. The plan was to try to get people talking again following the massive clampdown after internment. Harold Wilson and I both hoped that the agenda could be entirely open-ended, so that we could discuss the problems of the security of the Protestant majority as well as the SDLP's official ambition to secure unity for the whole of Ireland. It was my view at that time that such a conference would extend, with substantial periods for adjournment and consideration, over several months, and I still believe that if the initiative had been taken up actively and energetically that we might have made progress. But there was no lasting interest on Mr Maudling's side and eventually the idea faded out.

Faulkner came to London early in November for talks with Harold Wilson and me. He had been worried by rumours that the bi-partisan policy at Westminster was about to come to an end. Our discussion with him was pleasant but unproductive. I suppose it is possible that we could not get more movement in the political situation because the Army at this time were tentatively speculating that internment was beginning to work. They pointed to statistics that showed that whereas in September there had been an average of 225 incidents a week, that is riots, shootings and bombings, in October the number had fallen to 186 and by the end of November it was down to 160. I was appalled to discover that since August 9, a total of 1260 people had been arrested and detained for varying periods. This was gross over-reaction. The dragon's teeth were multiplying every week. Even so, and perhaps because of the number of arrests and detainees, recruits continued to be attracted to terrorist activity, and by the first week in December the tempo had quickened again. On December 5, in a most devastating single incident, 15 people, all Catholics, died in an explosion which demolished McGurk's Bar near the centre of Belfast. It brought the total death toll to 150. Twenty-three more people were to die before Christmas.

At about this time, I ceased for all practical purposes to be the Labour Party spokesman on Northern Ireland matters, and Merlyn Rees took over the day-to-day monitoring of events and shadowing Reginald Maudling. My last speech in the House on this issue was on November 29, 1971, following a massive opening of the debate by Harold Wilson in which he outlined his proposals for the reunification of Ireland based on a constitution which was to be determined by a commission comprising representatives of the United Kingdom Parliament, Stormont and the Parliament of the Republic, and which would not come into operation until 15 years after any agreement was concluded. He also proposed that as part of the settlement, the Irish Republic would join the Commonwealth and that Britain would provide financial aid to bring the Irish social security system up to United Kingdom standards. It was an imaginative speech which set the course of the whole two-day debate. But it was intended for long-range consumption and was not designed for immediate effect.

Merlyn Rees had seen something of the Northern Ireland situation in his ministerial capacity as an Under-Secretary at both the Ministry of Defence and the Home Office. His appointment to speak for the Parliamentary Party on this subject has justified itself in every particular and his success was recognized by his fellow Members of Parliament of the Labour Party in the autumn of 1972 when they elected him for the first time as a member of the Shadow Cabinet. When I dropped out of day-to-day contact with the tragic events of Northern Ireland, it was a great reassurance to know that Merlyn would be handling these matters for us.

This seems to be a suitable point to bring to an end the account of developments in Northern Ireland as I saw them. I was out of action in the early months of 1972, and suffice it to say that in the first three months up to March 24, 1972, when direct rule was introduced, the same relentless pattern of escalating violence and political stalemate continued.

By the middle of February the security forces had rounded up a total of 2447 people without stemming the tide of violence in any sense. On January 30 there was a confrontation between Catholics and paratroopers in Londonderry which resulted in the death of 13 men and boys. Early in March a bomb was placed in a busy restaurant in Belfast on a Saturday afternoon, killing two and injuring 136. And so the merciless killings went on, and still there was no sign of the Government's own political initiative which had been widely advertised as a package which would reconcile Protestant and Catholic.

Like many others, I felt despair and frustration at the absence of any political moves and after a headline appeared in *The Times* saying, 'Maudling refusal to be rushed on timing of Ulster initiative', I took the very rare step for me of writing to the Editor. 'What rush? When will the time arrive to act?' I asked. 'Further delay would only result in the situation continuing to get worse, week by week.' Because of the Government's irresolution I wrote: 'More and more of the authority that they should exercise is passing by default into the hands of Mr Faulkner.' I urged that the powers he was exercising were so rigorous and so wide that only the British Cabinet, responsible to Parliament, should employ them. Eventually, at long last, the Government did make up their minds to act.

Faulkner came to London to be told by Heath that the Government had now decided that it wanted internment to be phased out and control of security placed in Westminster's hands. Faulkner returned to Belfast to consult his Cabinet. When he flew back to London the message was clear. If responsibility for security was taken out of their hands, his Cabinet would resign as one man. It was. And they did. That was the beginning of direct rule.

13

Mr Maudling was replaced in March 1972 by William Whitelaw, who from the start injected into his task new energy, imagination and considerable political flair. He also enjoyed – as Maudling had – a favourable wind from the Labour Party. This was of outstanding importance in saving Northern Ireland, and perhaps the rest of the United Kingdom, from even worse bloodshed and misery, and made more possible the prospect of an enduring solution. Anyone who studies the history of Ireland from the mid-19th century onwards must conclude that – in marked contrast to the present stance of the major Parties – Irish problems were made much worse by the absence of any agreement between the Liberal and the Conservative Parties. Their differences were exaggerated by the cynical Tory attempt to exploit the Irish question as a British party issue, so that as one Government succeeded another, British policy towards Ireland seesawed to and fro. And always in the background stood a Conservative House of Lords to frustrate a Liberal majority in the Commons.

By contrast with today, Bonar Law, the leader of the Conservative Party in 1913, was reckless in his support of the para-military demonstrations held by the Protestants in Northern Ireland, and Conservatives openly supported the appointment of a retired British Major-General by the Ulster Unionists whose role was to command the Unionists in the armed conflict that they planned should follow the passage of the Home Rule Bill at Westminster. It was a disgraceful episode in the history of the Conservatives.

Thankfully, since the crisis of 1969, broad support for both Labour and Conservative Governments was forthcoming from the Opposition of the day and each Government was very conscious of the need to frame its policies so as to carry the Opposition with it in broad principle. This made the formation and execution of a consistent policy by Britain very much easier than it might have been.

To some extent this Parliamentary agreement was aided by the growing disgust of the general public with the cold-blooded murder and violence that took place. The public's impatient mood expressed itself in calls to withdraw the troops, to let the Irish cut each other's throats, and so on. This mood was resisted by both political parties and never reached dangerous levels. The attitude was very different in the days described by John Wilson in his *Life of Henry Campbell Bannerman*. Members of the Stock Exchange apparently marched to Guildhall, where they publicly burnt the Home Rule Bill to the singing of the National Anthem. When the Conservative House of Lords duly killed the Liberal Government's Bill, John Wilson recounts that the Peers emerged after the vote at 3.00 a.m. to be greeted by cheering crowds singing 'Rule, Britannia' and letting off fireworks. No one then objected to the Lords frustrating the intentions of the elected Commons.

The disillusion in the United Kingdom has its counterpart in Northern Ireland also. It takes the form of disenchantment with Westminster among the 'loyalist' Protestants. History shows that this hostility has always been latent, but it was concealed so long as Westminster sided with the Unionists in their disputes with the minority. It took the Unionists some time to recover from the shock of finding that neither the Labour Government nor public opinion in Britain backed them in 1969, but the Protestant working class became even more bitter when they discovered that a Conservative Government would not automatically back their demands either, and – even worse – insisted on interfering with, and finally suspending, Stormont. It is not enough for the 'loyalists' that both Parties adhere to the pledge that Northern Ireland must and will remain part of the United Kingdom for as long as that is the wish of a majority of the people. They hardly listen to what is said and even when they do, they refuse to be assured. Many half believe that eventually they will have to rely upon their own force of arms if they are to prevent themselves from being absorbed into the Republic.

In this they are wrong. Both Parties in Britain take very seriously the pledge that Northern Ireland shall not be handed over to the Republic. They mean what they say, not only because they have given the pledge and are morally bound to stand by it, but also because political leaders of both Parties in Britain, as well as those in the Republic, are aware of the bloody consequences that would follow a forcible re-unification. In my view the terrible bloodshed which took place in Belfast could then be transferred to Dublin, with extremist Protestant volunteers doing to that city what the IRA did in Belfast. So far as the pledge is concerned, violence in Belfast will not lead to unification – rather the reverse. I can think of only one circumstance in which the pledge to the majority might be withdrawn and that situation would arise from the actions of the majority themselves. I return to it later.

Another new factor to emerge since 1969 is that the Unionist disenchantment with the United Kingdom has been matched by a growing disappointment among the minority at the passive role played by the Republic during the disturbances. Apart from Lynch's original gesture of moving troops, he acted with great caution as the months went by. The Cosgrave/Corish Government shows no signs of being any more flamboyant. I have personally no doubt of the sincerity of the Republic when they say that, while re-unification remains an aspiration, it must be achieved by peaceful means. This clarification is healthy.

Another long-term hopeful result of the British refusal to back the ascendancy of the Ulster Unionist Party is that its monopoly power on Northern Ireland politics has been broken. It can never exercise the same complete grip over the life of Northern Ireland as it did during the first fifty years of the country's existence. In future the Unionists will have to share power with the minority, and if the Catholics seize the opportunity, there is a real prospect of peaceful development for both communities.

So despite the gloom, there are positive factors which, given good leadership by the politicians, can be turned to advantage. The politics of Northern Ireland have for too long been based on poisonous myths which are slowly being destroyed. If it is possible for good to come out of evil, then it could be that now both majority and minority know more clearly than ever before the reality of the attitude of Great Britain and the Republic of Ireland towards them, the leaders of both communities will perhaps realize that the people of Northern Ireland must look to themselves to work out their own salvation in co-operation with one another. And if they begin the process of

working together, they will find that each community possesses
unsuspected virtues.

But much depends upon the order of political priorities of the two
communities. Peace and progress does not mean that it will be necessary for the Catholic community to put aside the re-unification of
Ireland as their ultimate objective. What is required from them is
that they should cease to regard re-unification as the first priority to
which everything else takes second place. If the minority were to
decide to make economic reconstruction, jobs and housing their first
priority for the mid-term future, then a political partnership with
the majority would make sense. Conversely, the Protestants do not
need to give up their conception of a separate Northern Ireland. In
the mid-term future all that is required of them is that they should be
willing to share political power with the minority in order to achieve
the very necessary economic and other improvements in the life of
the people. It is not too much to expect.

A stumbling block in many Protestant eyes is the terms of the
Republic's Constitution, which in Article 2 declares the national
territory to be 'the whole island of Ireland, its islands and the territorial seas'. Article 3 asserts 'the right of Parliament and Government, established by this Constitution to exercise jurisdiction over
the whole of that territory'.

I have never been an admirer of written constitutions, whose rigidi-
ties can and do distort the natural growth of a nation and give much
less protection to the peoples' rights than they are supposed to do.
In the case of the Republic, the sentiments of its Constitution do not
represent the policies of the political parties; nevertheless, they give
extremist Unionists in the North a plausible reason for refusing to
work with the South. In an ideal world, I would like to see the Constitution rewritten so that while the Republic maintains its aspiration
to achieve a united Ireland in the fullness of time, it would renounce
its right to exercise its jurisdiction over the whole of Ireland. Is this
impossible? Only the citizens of the Republic can answer the question.
All I can say is that such a step would make it easier to discuss the
so-called 'Irish Dimension' and give the term a real meaning.

The British Government's White Paper on the constitutional proposals for Northern Ireland defined the Irish Dimension by saying
'that Northern Ireland is affected in numerous ways by what hap-

pened in the Republic of Ireland, and that the reverse is equally true.' The White Paper said that in making the point the Government was not making a political judgement but acknowledging an evident fact.

I referred in an earlier chapter to the occasion in Dublin in March 1971, when I revived the concept of an All-Ireland-Council, and that it met with a pretty cool response. Nevertheless, within two years, as the White Paper noted, virtually all the Northern Ireland political parties envisaged some sort of scheme for institutional arrangements between North and South and did not hesitate to use the term 'Council of Ireland'. In fairness I must add that there were different concepts of such a Council and in some cases the major emphasis was upon the conditions which would have to be met before it could operate successfully.

The British Government stated that it favoured and was prepared to facilitate the formation of such a body to consult and co-ordinate action, so it is worth while spending a moment to consider what its composition and functions might be.

First, as a Council it cannot be concerned with questions such as the unity of Ireland or the maintenance of the Border. Those matters are outside its competence. But it needs to be a meaningful body and will serve a useful purpose in institutionalizing relations and communication between North and South. It is also possible that its very existence will bring better understanding between majority and minority in the North. As to membership, on balance I would favour direct representation by some Ministers of the Government of the Republic and of the Executive from the North. In addition, the Council should include members of all major parties in the Dail and from the Assembly of Northern Ireland, but to prevent it from being wholly politically dominated, I would like to see included in its membership representatives of other institutions such as the trades unions, the Confederation of Irish Industry, the Confederation of British Industry and the farmers' organizations. Their presence would encourage discussion of matters of common economic concern such as regional development, industrial incentives, electricity generation and distribution, road networks and joint tourist promotion. I envisage a total membership of about 50, operating through the medium of standing separate commissions for different subjects but coming together for joint discussion from time to time. No doubt as confidence grew, other commissions drawn from the Council's ranks would suggest themselves, and I would like to see one devoted to an early examination of educational problems, starting perhaps with the teaching of history and the exchange of teachers.

The Council of Ireland must have a permanent secretariat to provide continuity in its work and to take the initiative in proposing subjects for examination that are of concern to both North and South. The commissions might perhaps take a leaf out of the book of the European Parliament and invite Ministers who are not members to appear before them in order to give an account of their policies. The commissions should also be able to ask the two governments for observations on policies they are following.

These kinds of activity would improve communication and understanding between North and South, but equally they would lead sooner rather than later to the cry that the All Ireland Council was no more than a talking shop. If that criticism came from both North and South, then clearly it could and should be met by conceding some powers to the Council. But it would be fatal to do so unless there was clear agreement from both sides of the Border. There will be certain difficulties to overcome because the Assembly, unlike the Dail, is not a sovereign Parliament. Logically, that might lead to the proposal that the United Kingdom should be a member of the Council – to which I would be opposed. However, if both parties desired the United Kingdom to have some link short of full membership, then I would see advantages in Britain sending observers to the Council and commissions, at any rate in the early years of their existence.

Another problem which needs to be worked over (but not initially by the All-Ireland Council) is how the basic civil rights of every person are to be guaranteed, whether he lives in the Republic or the North. This is a most difficult question. Would Parliament at Westminster, the Assembly in Belfast and the Dail in Dublin be willing to agree to the creation of a new Constitutional Court charged with such a task? If so, what should be the manner of appointment of the judges and from whom would they derive their authority?

I raise these questions without attempting to answer them, for they are beyond my competence. A number of possible solutions have been suggested but the important point is that, given proper safeguards, the authority of such a Constitutional Court could be a powerful reassurance to both minority and majority in the North.

On purely internal issues, the problem for the Assembly of Northern Ireland is whether there will emerge from it an Executive capable of agreeing on a programme of radical, progressive policies to meet the basic social and economic needs. They start from the point that Northern Ireland is the least prosperous region of the United Kingdom. It has the highest percentage of men and women unemployed. Its people have the lowest average income per head and the smallest output per head in the United Kingdom. In social terms the degree of poverty in some parts of the North is so great that half the families in which there is a full-time working breadwinner still have wages below the supplementary benefit level.

Northern Ireland's prosperity depends upon public investment to a much greater extent than private investment, and an active policy of setting up state-owned industries is vital if the intolerably high rate of unemployment is to be reduced. A useful instrument would be a Reconstruction Corporation to take the initiative in searching for new industries whose product is needed in the market. It should have at its disposal a financial institution such as a credit bank to assist both agriculture and industry with loans and other facilities at preferential rates.

The Assembly should also look once again at the marketing and purchasing agencies in the important area of agriculture. Eighty per cent of the feeding stuffs required by Northern Ireland livestock and dairy farmers are imported, and an early examination should be made of the need for special agencies to negotiate bulk purchase and bulk imports of feeding stuffs in order to strengthen the bargaining power of the small farmer and to encourage co-operative arrangements between farmers. This, too, is a field in which a Standing Commission of the All Ireland Council could be invaluable.

Another priority field for decision and action by the Assembly and Executive is education. The Northern Ireland Advisory Council on Education issued a Report in February 1973 calling, by a majority, for the elimination of selection at 11-plus and further recommending, as a matter of urgency, development schemes on the basis of comprehensive education in mixed areas where Catholics and Protestants reside together. The Committee's view was that it would be unrealistic to expect the introduction of integrated schools in the near future, but they report that in some schools there is already mixing at staff and pupil level and that development of this depends very largely on the attitudes and decisions of parents. They recommended an increase in the arrangements by which schools of different denominational character collaborate, such as discussions between pupil groups, career exhibitions and school leavers' conferences, country or seaside holidays, shared camps or hostels and community service. Comprehensive education may take a long time to become established in Northern Ireland, but it should be the policy of a progressive, radical administration to proceed by way of integrating classes at the senior level and by means of exchanges of teachers between Protestant and Catholic schools. The teaching of history and the nature of the syllabus is something which needs urgent consideration. The beneficial result of this kind of work lies many years in the future but it needs a dynamic thrust now.

While the future control of the police is rightly reserved to Westminster for the time being, this should not be regarded as the ultimate solution. If the Northern Ireland Executive and Assembly can succeed and non-sectarian parties become the regular pattern for government there, then Westminster should be willing, in due course, to hand back control of the police. The police are more suitable to fulfil the task of maintaining order than the army with its frequent postings, for the most successful police force is one that is a part of the whole community and enjoys its confidence. For this reason, despite the Hunt Commission reforms, there is a case for Westminster to look once again at the structure of the Royal Ulster Constabulary in order to examine the possibility of separate, locally based forces under suitable control as a better way of policing particular areas in the Province.

One danger that must be guarded against with the establishment of a new Assembly and Executive is the temptation for the Secretary of State at Westminster to allow his control over the situation to slip gradually away. Even in the case of the powers that are prescribed for the Executive, it is important that oversight by the Secretary of State should be continuous. As to the Secretary of State's own powers, we should learn the lesson of the 1920s and 1930s and not allow them to be eroded, either by inertia on our part or as a result of aggrandizement by the Northern Ireland Executive. If there is to be future change in the powers exercised by Westminster and Belfast respectively, let the changes be made deliberately and formally.

I have outlined the kind of Northern Ireland that I would like to see emerge from the present situation and it is not an impossible vision. But everything depends upon bringing to an end the state of violence and defeating both the IRA and the Protestant extremists. To that end, the army must continue their efforts and remain for as long as is necessary to bring the situation under control. But as soon as possible they must hand over their responsibilities to a strengthened and reformed police force.

Until this is settled, it is difficult to say how politics will develop. The trades unions are the main channel for providing a non-sectarian meeting point for both communities and should be able to exert more muscle in the political field. I would like to see them provide the basis for the Northern Ireland Labour Party, but events have shown that non-sectarian parties will only thrive when inter-communal tension is lowered.

As long as Britain is satisfied that the majority of the population accepts the final sovereignty of the Westminster Parliament, then it will unquestionably hold to its responsibilities to the majority on the Border question, and to the minority in ensuring their basic civil rights and a fair share in the government of the Province. But I cannot conclude without saying that a new situation would arise if there was intransigence among the majority of Northern Ireland politicians elected to the Assembly. If, at any time, the Assembly and the Executive should be made unworkable through a deliberate refusal by the majority to play their part, then in my judgement the United Kingdom would be entitled to reconsider her position and her pledges on all matters. If a majority of the elected representatives of the Northern Ireland people are in the end unwilling to accept the sovereignty of Westminster, then they have no right and no title to demand either the help or the protection of the British Government. Westminster has made a compact, costly and difficult to carry out, and fraught with danger. Britain cannot be expected to adhere to it unless the majority in Northern Ireland fulfil their part of the bargain too. If such a problem arose because politicians made the constitution of Northern Ireland unworkable, I would recommend the Government of the day to call a round table conference of all parties at

Westminster and associate with it those in the North who were prepared to co-operate. At a suitable stage the Republic of Ireland would need to be brought into consultation also. An All Party Conference would be the most likely way to forge a new national approach. If we were forced to hold such a Conference, the Labour and Conservative Parties, with others, would be free to reconsider the future of Northern Ireland from the point of view of where Britain's best interests lie and to reach what conclusions they thought best both for Britain and Northern Ireland.

So if, by sabotage of the political structure of Northern Ireland, the majority deliberately contracted out, then Britain should feel morally free to reconsider the link between herself and Northern Ireland, the provision of troops to Northern Ireland and the financial subsidy to the Province. No one could forecast what conclusions might be reached, for much would depend on the prevailing circumstances and I most strongly hope that such a calamity will not occur. But Britain cannot be expected to sit patiently and bleed indefinitely if her best efforts face deliberate sabotage by the elected majority of the Province.

One last question remains to be answered. Do I wish or do I expect to see a united Ireland some time in the future? And I answer such a question as honestly as I can: I do not know whether it will come. I do know that it can only come through a freely negotiated voluntary agreement. I recognize that the South has been long separated from a large part of the North by religion, by education, and to some extent by culture, and that before unity can be more than a dream, North and South will need to develop the habit of working together on matters of common interest. If as a result they learn to trust each other, each community may see the other in a new light.

So, at the end of the day, I would like to see Ireland come together again. If and when it does, it will be a signal to the world that the people themselves have freely entered into a new compact because they are at peace and at ease with one another and recognize how much they have in common. If, as I hope, that time comes, the rest of us will rejoice that the warm-hearted qualities of generosity and courage, found in both communities, have finally outweighed their differences.

THE DOWNING STREET
COMMUNIQUE
AND DECLARATION

A meeting was held at No. 10 Downing Street this evening between the Prime Minister, Mr Harold Wilson, the Foreign and Commonwealth Secretary, Mr Michael Stewart, the Home Secretary, Mr James Callaghan, the Secretary of State for Defence, Mr Denis Healey, and the Minister of State at the Home Office, Lord Stonham, and the Prime Minister of Northern Ireland, Major Chichester-Clark, the Deputy Prime Minister, Mr J. L. O. Andrews, the Minister of Home Affairs, Mr R. W. Porter, and the Minister of Development, Mr Brian Faulkner.

In a six-hour discussion the whole situation in Northern Ireland was reviewed. It was agreed that the GOC Northern Ireland will with immediate effect assume overall responsibility for security operations. He will continue to be responsible directly to the Ministry of Defence but will work in the closest co-operation with the Northern Ireland Government and the Inspector-General of the Royal Ulster Constabulary. For all security operations the GOC will have full control of the deployment and tasks of the Royal Ulster Constabulary. For normal police duties outside the field of security the Royal Ulster Constabulary will remain answerable to the Inspector-General who will be responsible to the Northern Ireland Government.

The GOC will assume full command and control of the Ulster Special Constabulary for all purposes including their organization, deployment, tasks and arms. Their employment by the Northern Ireland Government in riot and crowd control was always envisaged as a purely temporary measure. With the increased deployment of the Army and the assumption by the GOC of operational control of all the security forces, it will be possible for the Special Constabulary to be progressively and rapidly relieved of these temporary duties at his discretion, starting in the cities. The question of the custody of Special Constabulary arms will similarly be within his discretion. Consideration will be given to the problem of country areas and the defence of vital public service installations.

The Northern Ireland Ministers agreed that an appeal should be made to all members of the public to hand in unauthorized weapons under an amnesty.

In order that British troops can be withdrawn from the internal security role at the earliest possible moment the two Governments will discuss as a matter of urgency the future of the civilian security services of Northern Ireland which will take over when the troops withdraw.

Major Chichester-Clark said that it was the intention of the Northern Ireland Government to set up forthwith an impartial investigation into the recent grave public disorders. Further details will be announced very shortly by the Northern Ireland Minister of Home Affairs.

The United Kingdom Ministers proposed and the Northern Ireland Ministers readily agreed that two senior civil servants from London should be temporarily stationed with the Northern Ireland Government in Belfast to represent the increased concern which the United Kingdom Government had necessarily acquired in Northern Ireland affairs through the commitment of the Armed Forces in the present conditions.

The question of detainees was discussed.

The two Governments agreed to a joint Declaration on the principles which should govern their future actions.

The Ministers agreed to meet again early in September.

10 Downing Street, S.W.1
19th August, 1969

DECLARATION

1. The United Kingdom Government reaffirm that nothing which has happened in recent weeks in Northern Ireland derogates from the clear pledges made by successive United Kingdom Governments that Northern Ireland should not cease to be a part of the United Kingdom without the consent of the people of Northern Ireland or from the provision in Section I of the Ireland Act, 1949, that in no event will Northern Ireland or any part thereof cease to be part of the United Kingdom without the consent of the Parliament of Northern Ireland. The border is not an issue.

2. The United Kingdom Government again affirm that responsibility for affairs in Northern Ireland is entirely a matter of domestic jurisdiction. The United Kingdom Government will take full responsibility for asserting this principle in all international relationships.

3. The United Kingdom Government have ultimate responsibility for the protection of those who live in Northern Ireland when, as in the past week, a breakdown of law and order has occurred. In this spirit, the United Kingdom Government responded to the requests of the Northern Ireland Government for military assistance in Londonderry and Belfast in order to restore law and order. They emphasize again that troops will be withdrawn when law and order has been restored.

4. The Northern Ireland Government have been informed that troops have been provided on a temporary basis in accordance with the United Kingdom's ultimate responsibility. In the context of the commitment of these troops, the Northern Ireland Government have reaffirmed their intention to take into the fullest account at all times the views of Her Majesty's Government in the United Kingdom, especially in relation to matters affecting the status of citizens of that part of the United Kingdom and their equal rights and protection under the law.

5. The United Kingdom Government have welcomed the decisions of the Northern Ireland Government relating to local government franchise, the revision of local government areas, the allocation of houses, the creation of a Parliamentary Commissioner for Admini-

stration in Northern Ireland and machinery to consider citizens' grievances against other public authorities which the Prime Minister reported to the House of Commons at Westminster following his meeting with Northern Ireland Ministers on 21st May as demonstrating the determination of the Northern Ireland Government that there shall be full equality of treatment for all citizens. Both Governments have agreed that it is vital that the momentum of internal reform should be maintained.

6. The two Governments at their meeting at 10 Downing Street today have reaffirmed that in all legislation and executive decisions of Government every citizen of Northern Ireland is entitled to the same equality of treatment and freedom from discrimination as obtains in the rest of the United Kingdom, irrespective of political views or religion. In their further meetings the two Governments will be guided by these mutually accepted principles.

7. Finally, both Governments are determined to take all possible steps to restore normality to the Northern Ireland community so that economic development can proceed at the faster rate which is vital for social stability.

10 Downing Street, S.W.1
19th August, 1969

DISTURBANCES IN NORTHERN IRELAND

Extract from the Report of the Cameron Commission to the Governor of Northern Ireland, September 1969. (Cmd 532.)

SUMMARY OF CONCLUSIONS ON CAUSES OF DISORDERS

229. Having carried out as full an investigation as lay within our competence we can summarize our conclusions upon the immediate and precipitating causes of the disorders which broke out in Londonderry on October 5, 1968, and continued thereafter both in Londonderry and elsewhere on subsequent dates. These are both general and particular.

(a) General

(1) A rising sense of continuing injustice and grievance among large sections of the Catholic population in Northern Ireland, in particular in Londonderry and Dungannon, in respect of (i) inadequacy of housing provision by certain local authorities (ii) unfair methods of allocation of houses built and let by such authorities, in particular, refusals and omissions to adopt a 'points' system in determining priorities and making allocations (iii) misuse in certain cases of discretionary powers of allocation of houses in order to perpetuate Unionist control of the local authority.

(2) Complaints, now well documented in fact, of discrimination in the making of local government appointments, at all levels but especially in senior posts, to the prejudice of non-Unionists and especially Catholic members of the community, in some Unionist controlled authorities.

(3) Complaints, again well documented, in some cases of

193

deliberate manipulation of local government electoral boundaries and in others a refusal to apply for their necessary extension, in order to achieve and maintain Unionist control of local authorities and so to deny to Catholics influence in local government proportionate to their numbers.

(4) A growing and powerful sense of resentment and frustration among the Catholic population at failure to achieve either acceptance on the part of the Government of any need to investigate these complaints or to provide and enforce a remedy for them.

(5) Resentment, particularly among Catholics, as to the existence of the Ulster Special Constabulary (the B-Specials) as a partisan and paramilitary force recruited exclusively from Protestants.

(6) Widespread resentment among Catholics in particular at the continuance in force of regulations made under the Special Powers Act, and of the continued presence in the statute book of the Act itself.

(7) Fears and apprehensions among Protestants of a threat to Unionist domination and control of Government by increase of Catholic population and powers, inflamed in particular by the activities of the Ulster Constitution Defence Committee and the Ulster Protestant Volunteers, provoked strong hostile reaction to civil rights claims as asserted by the Civil Rights Association and later by the People's Democracy which was readily translated into physical violence against Civil Rights demonstrators.

(b) *Particular*

(8) There was a strong reaction of popular resentment to the Minister's ban on the route of the proposed Civil Rights march in Londonderry on October 5, 1968, which swelled very considerably the number of persons who ultimately took part in the march. Without this ban the numbers taking part would in all probability have been small and the situation safely handled by available police forces.

(9) The leadership, organization and control of the demonstrations in Londonderry on October 5, 1968, and in Newry on January 11, 1969, was ineffective and insufficient to prevent violent or disorderly conduct among certain elements present on these occasions.

(10) There was early infiltration of the Civil Rights Association both centrally and locally by subversive left wing and revolutionary elements which were prepared to use the Civil Rights movement to further their own purposes, and were ready to exploit grievances in order to provoke and foment, and did provoke and foment, disorder and violence in the guise of supporting a non-violent movement.

(11) This infiltration was assisted by the declared insistence of the Civil Rights Association that it was non-sectarian and non-political, and its consequent refusal to reject support from whatever quarter it came provided that support was given and limited to the published aims of the Association.

(12) What was originally a Belfast students' protest against police action in Londonderry on October 5 and support for the Civil Rights movement was transformed into the People's Demo-cracy – itself an unnecessary adjunct to the already existing and operative Civil Rights Association. People's Democracy provided a means by which politically extreme and militant elements could and did invite and incite civil disorder, with the consequence of polarizing and hardening opposition to Civil Rights claims.

(13) On the other side the deliberate and organized interventions by followers of Major Bunting and the Rev. Dr Paisley, especially in Armagh, Burntollet and Londonderry, substantially increased the risk of violent disorder on occasions when Civil Rights demonstrations or marches were to take place, were a material contributory cause of the outbreaks of violence which occurred after October 5, and seriously hampered the police in their task of maintaining law and order, and of protecting members of the public in the exercise of their undoubted legal rights and upon their lawful occasions.

(14) The police handling of the demonstration in Londonderry on October 5, 1968, was in certain material respects ill co-ordinated and inept. There was use of unnecessary and ill-controlled force in the dispersal of the demonstrators, only a minority of whom acted in a disorderly and violent manner. The wide publicity given by press, radio and television to particular episodes inflamed and exacerbated feelings of resentment against the police which had been already aroused by their enforcement of the ministerial ban.

(15) Available police forces did not provide adequate protection to People's Democracy marchers at Burntollet Bridge and in or near Irish Street, Londonderry on January 4, 1969. There were instances of police indiscipline and violence towards persons unassociated with rioting or disorder on 4-5 January in Londonderry and these provoked serious hostility to the police, particularly among the Catholic population of Londonderry, and an increasing disbelief in their impartiality towards non-Unionists.

(16) Numerical insufficiency of available police force especially in Armagh on November 30, 1968, and in Londonderry on January 4-5, 1969, and later on April 19-20 prevented early and complete control and, where necessary, arrest of disorderly and riotous elements.

The Government's announcements on the reform of local government franchise – the 'one man one vote' issue – reform and readjustment of local government administration, including electoral areas and boundaries, introduction of a comprehensive and fair 'points' system in the allocation of Council built houses and the introduction of special machinery to deal with complaints arising out of matters of local administration, go a very considerable way, not only to acknowledge the justice of the complaints on these points but also the expediency and necessity of providing remedies for them.

Paras. 230 *and* 231 *dealt with procedures for investigating complaints against the police, and the manner of appointment of senior local authority officials.*

232. Looking back on the course of this Inquiry and of all its implications we feel bound to express our very firm conviction, based on the extent and weight of the evidence and opinions presented to us and collected by us, that the honest implementation of these reforms already promised or foreshadowed by the Government with the least necessary delay, is one essential step towards the development of a lasting peace and a measure of harmony and mutual understanding among all the people of Northern Ireland. There are, as we are well aware, other and difficult elements in the community's problems which statesmanship has to solve, but we have been left with no doubt that without these reforms and changes there would be grave risk of further and more serious disorders in the future which, if they occurred, would inevitably rouse more bitter and more

irreconcilable passions on either side. It was fortunate indeed that, for whatever cause, the disorders into which we have inquired over the past months, serious as they were, were not made even more grave by resort to the use of firearms – except on two isolated happily accompanied by no injury to persons or property. Unhappily this can no longer be said of the events which have occurred so tragically during the preparation of this Report.

233. We have endeavoured as fairly and as fully as we could to investigate the matters remitted to us and have now submitted our conclusions and the reasons which have led to them. Our inquiry has disclosed many deep rooted causes of dissension and of bitter memories, many matters which must be a cause of distress to all who have the interest of Northern Ireland, its prosperity and that of its people at heart. At the same time there have been encouraging signs that attitudes among Unionists and non-Unionists alike were and had been undergoing change and modification, and that extremist views on either side were becoming more isolated and commanding less support. It would however be a grave political and social error to regard the Civil Rights movement as narrowly sectarian or subversively political; it was and is a movement which drew – and still draws – support from a wide measure of moderate opinion on many sides and to that extent is a novel phenomenon in the political firmament of Northern Ireland.

234. Finally we express the hope that in the discharge of our task we have succeeded in placing the true facts in their proper perspective, in analysing the numerous contributory and conflicting causes of these disorders, in strengthening the support which the measures the Government has announced to repair grievances and remedy justifiable grievances can command, and that in so doing this Report may in some degree serve to promote the cause of peace and mutual understanding among all the people of Northern Ireland.

235. Since this Report was drafted and during the period of its preparation, certain events of grave disorder, in particular in Belfast and Londonderry, have occurred, which go far to confirm the inference which we have already drawn in earlier parts of our Report, that there have been and are at work within Northern Ireland persons whose immediate and deliberate intention is to prepare, plan and provoke violence, reckless of the consequences to persons or property.

Their purpose is not to secure peace by way of reform and within structure of the state. At the same time, there are others who by their appeal to sectarian prejudices and bigotry have assisted to inflame passions and keep alive ancient hatreds that have readily led to the unleashing of lawless and uncontrolled violence. From the aimless and vicious hooligans of the streets and alleys to the extremists of right or left, of whatever creed, Catholic or Protestant, all would appear to bear a share of blame for the tragic events which have occurred and in which the vast majority of the population of Northern Ireland have neither hand nor concern and which we have no doubt they most deeply deplore.

236. In a situation which contains so many grave possibilities we would again draw particular attention to the complexity of the causes of those disorders which we were called on to investigate, and to the dangers which over-emphasis or over-simplification in press or other report or comment on particular facets of these causes could so readily produce. These unhappy events have already received very wide press and television coverage which, as we have observed, sometimes highlighted intentionally or by chance particular incidents the reporting of which may well have distorted or tended to distort the accuracy of the picture of the whole.

John Cameron
J. Henry Biggart
J. J. Campbell

August 16, 1969

COMMUNIQUE

Issued at end of visit of Home Secretary to Northern Ireland
August 27-9, 1969

During his visit to Belfast, the Home Secretary, Mr James Callaghan, was invited to attend two meetings with the Northern Ireland Cabinet, on 27th and 29th August; at the second meeting the Home Secretary was accompanied by the Minister of State, Home Office, Lord Stonham.

2. Her Majesty's Government in the United Kingdom have reaffirmed the pledges previously given that Northern Ireland will remain a part of the United Kingdom as long as its Parliament and people so wish, and have assured the Northern Ireland Government that this position is unaffected by recent events.

3. The Home Secretary noted two measures already taken as being of particular importance in the restoration of confidence: the establishment in pursuance of Resolutions by the Northern Ireland Parliament of a tribunal of inquiry under the chairmanship of Mr Justice Scarman to inquire into the recent grave disorders; and by the Northern Ireland Government of an Advisory Board, under the chairmanship of Lord Hunt, to examine the recruitment, organization, structure and composition of the Royal Ulster Constabulary and Ulster Special Constabulary and their respective functions: and to recommend, as necessary, what changes are required to provide for the efficient enforcement of law and order in Northern Ireland. The necessity for an early report was emphasized on both sides.

4. The Northern Ireland Ministers reported to the Home Secretary on the progress being made with the reforms already announced. They informed him that in addition to legislation already passed to establish a Parliamentary Commissioner in Northern Ireland, they intend to introduce legislation to establish machinery for the investigation of citizens' grievances against local authorities or other public authorities. This legislation would embody, as an ultimate sanction, provision for remedies in the courts. They explained that

the points scheme for the allocation of local authority houses was now in operation in all local authority areas pending consideration by the Minister of Development of the comments of particular authorities on the application of such schemes in their areas. Thereafter the Minister would approve permanent schemes only if they were based on this principle.

Attention was drawn to the Northern Ireland Government's White Paper on Reshaping of Local Government Reform published in July which embodied firm proposals for the designation by an independent body of the electoral divisions within the new local government areas. The latter proposal will be implemented by legislation this Session.

The Home Secretary also noted the Northern Ireland Government's decision to introduce legislation to set up a Community Relations Board to promote good relations between all sections of the community. Half the members of the Board would be Protestant and half Roman Catholic.

5. Recognizing as they do the need to maintain the momentum of reform, Northern Ireland Ministers intend to consider the accelerated recall of Parliament to press on with measures which are now being prepared, with a view to their early enactment.

6. The Northern Ireland Ministers informed the Home Secretary that apart from four persons who were being charged with criminal offences all detainees had been released.

The Home Secretary informed the Northern Ireland Cabinet that the United Kingdom Government had agreed to make a grant of £250,000 in order to relieve the present distress in Northern Ireland. It will be used:

(a) To relieve the immediate distress of individuals by providing clothing, food, medical care and essential furniture (e.g. beds, bedding and cooking utensils).

(b) To spread the money as far as possible to satisfy the most urgent needs.

(c) To provide a small cash grant where provision in kind is not appropriate.

The grant will take the form of a contribution to the Ulster Innocent Victims Appeal Fund.

7. In their discussions Ministers had very much in mind the

affirmation in paragraph 6 of the joint Declaration made at Downing Street on 19th August, of the entitlement of every citizen of Northern Ireland to the same equality of treatment and freedom from discrimination as obtains in the rest of the United Kingdom, irrespective of political views or religion.

8. It has been agreed that effective action in the following fields is fundamental to the creation of confidence:

(i) Equality of opportunity for all in public employment, without regard to religious or political considerations.

(ii) Protection against the incitement of hatred against any citizen on the grounds of religious belief.

(iii) Guaranteed fairness in the allocation of public authority housing, with need, assessed by objective criteria, as the only relevant yardstick.

(iv) Effective means not only for the investigation of grievances against public bodies, but for their ultimate redress if conciliation and other procedures are ineffective.

(v) Proper representation of minorities, to be assured at the elected levels of government by completely fair electoral laws, practices and boundaries, and at nominated or appointed levels by a recognition that such minorities have a right to an effective voice in affairs.

9. The Government of Northern Ireland have accordingly sought the co-operation of the Home Secretary in setting up joint working parties of officials of the two Governments to examine the extent to which the Government of Northern Ireland's present practice or pledged commitments adequately ensure

(i) the fair allocation of houses by public authorities;

(ii) the avoidance of any discrimination in any form of public employment; and

(iii) the promotion of good community relations by methods including the prohibition of incitement to religious hatred

and to report to the Government of Northern Ireland within a matter of weeks.

10. To mark the great importance he attaches to the promotion of good community relations the Prime Minister of Northern Ireland has intimated his intention to designate a Minister with special responsibility for that subject.

11. At the request of the Northern Ireland Government a mission of representatives from United Kingdom Departments concerned with economic and social affairs (including the Ministry of Technology, the Board of Trade and the Department of Economic Affairs) will visit Northern Ireland at a very early date to assess the economic and industrial prospects in the light of recent events.

12. The Home Secretary assured Northern Ireland Ministers of the readiness of himself and his colleagues to help in any way possible in any steps that would lead to a better life for the whole community in Northern Ireland, and to an elimination of the root causes of many of the grievances which have been expressed.

13. The Home Secretary joined with the Northern Ireland Cabinet in appealing to all citizens of Northern Ireland to use their influence to restore harmony between all sections of the community in the interests of the well-being and prosperity of the Province. The Home Secretary said that speedy implementation of the reforms already announced and action following the further studies would go far to reduce tension and restore confidence and deserved a co-operative response from all sections of the community in Northern Ireland.

14. The Home Secretary readily accepted the invitation of the Northern Ireland Cabinet to pay another visit to Belfast in mid-October for discussion of the conclusions reached by the working parties and of the action to be taken as a result of the report of the Advisory Board on the police.

29th August 1969

Index